CW00766249

The Magic Seeker's Guide to the Design Universe

In *Designers Universe - The WOW Factor*, we spotlight 59 professional designers who shine within the field. They come from different corners of the world, specializing in various fields such as graphic design, illustration, fashion, set design, and motion graphics, but they all have one thing in common: there is a unique aesthetic which they try to convey through their work, which sets them apart from other designers.

It has been a year since we sent out the first invitation letter to the designers we wished to include in this project. During this time, we talked to over a hundred designers from every continent, reviewed about a thousand pieces of works and finally settled on these 59 "WOW"-inspiring designers. Although the process of

WHEN YOU
LINK GOOD
IDEAS WITH
BRAVE PEOPLE,
IT CAN BE
MAGIC.

DESIGNERS UNIVERSE
THE WOW FACTOR

ISBN 978-1-58423-475-3

First Published in the United States of America by Gingko Press
by arrangement with Sandu Publishing Co., Limited

Gingko Press, Inc.
1321 Fifth Street
Berkeley, CA 94710 USA
Tel: (510) 898 1195
Fax: (510) 898 1196
Email: books@gingkopress.com
www.gingkopress.com

SANDU⊜ | 360°

Copyright © 2011 by SANDU PUBLISHING

Sponsored by: Design 360° – Concept and Design Magazine
Chief Editor: Wang Shaoqiang
Executive Editor: Yvonne Syan Yi
Chief Designer: Wang Shaoqiang
Book Designer: Leo Cheung
Sales Managers:
Niu Guanghui (China), Daniela Huang (International)
Address:
3rd Floor, West Tower,
No.10 Ligang Road, Haizhu District,
510280, Guangzhou, China
Tel: (86)-20-84344460
Fax: (86)-20-84344460
sandu.sales@gmail.com
www.sandu360.com

All rights reserved. No part of this publication may be reproduced
or transmitted in any form or by any means, electronic or
mechanical, including photocopy, recording or any information
storage and retrieval system, without prior permission in writing
from the publisher.

Printed and bound in China

selecting images and conducting interviews was daunting, we worked together with all of the contributors to create an outstanding design collection. We hope that when you open this book, you not only enjoy the exceptional creative output of the featured designers, but also that you draw inspiration from their views on design and life. May their wonderful stories and work add richness to your day, and help you to create your own magic.

Editor

What Does a Leading-edge Designer Look Like?

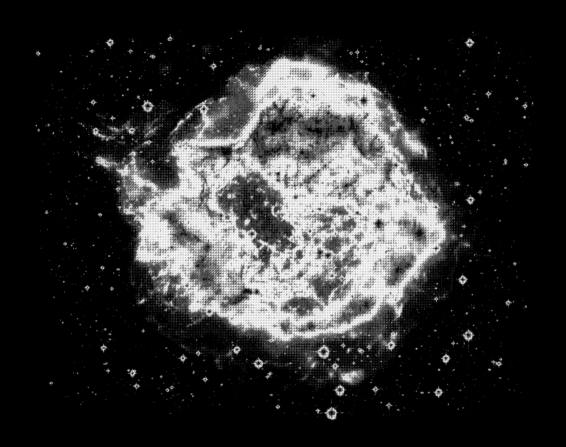

Single-breasted   Double-breasted

He has an open heart, aiming for the sky with he's felt on the ground.

He never STOPS Dreaming!

OCULOS de SOLDAR   LÁPIS   CADERNO

FILME   FREE LIBERDADE

THAT'S A REALLY DIFFICULT QESTION. MAYBE LIKE A YOUNG BOB DYLAN, A VISIONARY, SELF MADE PERSON AND A WAYWARD.

If there was a look that a leading-edge designer had,
I would want to have that look — as long as it didn't involve
plastic surgery.

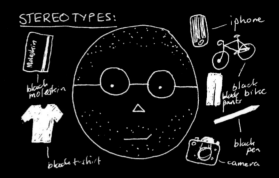

STEREOTYPES:
- Moleskin / black moleskin
- iphone
- black bike pants
- black pen
- black t-shirt
- camera

WHAT DOES A LEADING-EDGE DESIGNER LOOK LIKE?

FREESTYLE

**A HEAD,
A BODY,
TWO ARMS,
TWO LEGS,
AND A MAC BOOK PRO**

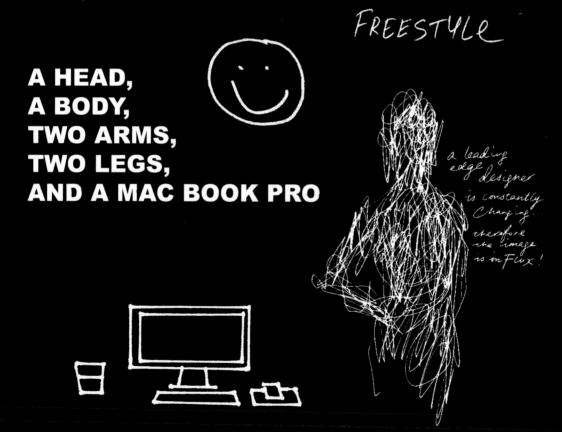

a leading edge designer is constantly changing... therefore the image is in Flux!

He usually has a beard, very tired during the week and looks a bit nerdy.

No ideas. But I believe he must be very passionate in design and always have a curiosity to explore new things.

Creative
Intuitive
Experimental
Not afraid of break "rules"

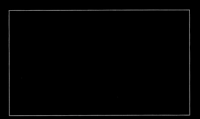

"I don't think I can define a boundary. The frame, you gave me, that is enough."

I think there is not standard model for a leading-edge designer. I know designers who dress in a classic way despite being up-to-date and others dress casual, some others dress more elegant wearing suits and ties. It depends on your likes!

I try to be comfortable as long as I spend many hours on the computer. I wear comfortable shirt, jeans and sneakers.

Antwort (Bild):

A greedy animal playing and jumping among designs to find the extraordinary one. A Panda trying to escape from the standard design world.

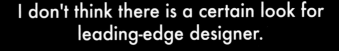

I don't think there is a certain look for leading-edge designer.

I'm going to choose David Pearson as my idea of what a leading edge designer looks like, I think he does some amazing, beautiful and innovative work, but it also connects to a really wide audience, which I think is important. Good design shouldn't be esoteric; it should be able to connect with people from all walks of life.

I think leading-edge designers depend on the project, for example: concept and applications. Nowadays, what I like most is experimental editorial design. In my magazine "Nofreno" (about fixed bikes) I let myself play with the images. If you have noticed, in some pages they are looking down. That's because the concept (based on dynamic and movement) allows us to create this kind of things.

I guess there is no typical way of looking. At least i can't think of a specific way a creative should look like. Of course there are some sorts of stereotypes but actually the outer appearance of a designer does not matter at all as long as he/she is able to think outside the box and be creative.

Like nothing in particular.

That's a really difficult question. Maybe like a young Bob Dylan; a visionary, self made person and a way ward.

It seems that they all wear black frame glasses.

A leader edge designer is a Chameleon, changing his/her accent and walk to suit the problems they're confronted with.

"Imaginative mind"

Computer<Brain

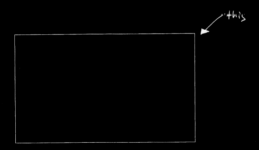

← this

Samuel Egloff and Catrina Wipf

Definitely not like a leading-edge designer.

To begin with, I just want to say that I'm not that fond of spotting out stereotypes. I mean, of course there are certain codes and trends in the design world of how a designer should and wants to look, but I always get surprised when I meet a really good designer and they are never what you expect. I think designers in general are questioning everything around them and that's also been my way of finding new ideas, because faces it. It's not how you look that is important, it's how you perceive the world and how that reflects on your work that I find interesting about people. Not how they dress.

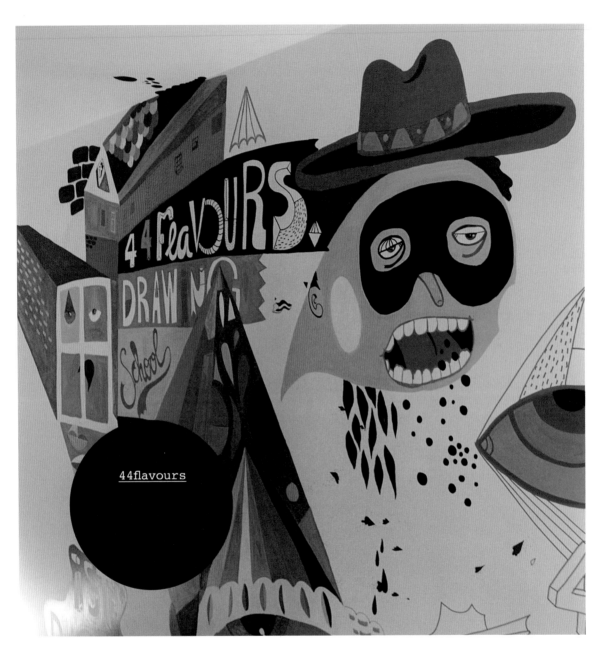

44flavours

44flavours is an art collective based in Kreuzberg - Berlin, consisting of Sebastian Bagge and Julio Rölle.

44flavours's work showcases a high level of knowledge of the diverse fields of art, by incorporating and rearranging them to bring their own visions to life.

Growing up with graffiti and the derivative sample and remix culture of hip-hop, both artists developed their individual styles without the implicit limits of any specific medium - instead they exploited multiple media to support and best express their ideas and tastes at the moment of creation.

44flavours is not only synonymous with strangely beautiful exhibitions, which frequently sprout up all over Europe, but also with a cutting edge design studio, which focuses on a very broad scope of graphic design, illustration and typography.

44flavours is still evolving in an environment of unlimited freedom and creativity. Their studio activity is dedicated to pushing skill, craft and conceptual knowledge to their ever widening limits.

How did you get the name "44flavours"?

The name comes from one of those Brooklyn ice cream vans you can see all over the hood in the summer, which we saw in some film. And no joke - it really was called 44flavours! The name was perfect because that was exactly what we wanted to show people when we decided to start a magazine 7 years ago - different flavours concentrated in one format. And then to top

it off, no matter how you write the name it's always typographically dope! Finally we ended up using this name for our design bureau as well as for the art collective: 44flavours!

look of those old storefront signs from back in the day – the ones that were really hand painted. The craziest thing we did recently was artificially ageing the wood that we used to build our letterforms. We primed it, painted it with different paints, sanded it down, repainted it, sanded it down again, rubbed soil into it, poured coffee over it, then painted it again – and finally we screen printed and painted our designs over

that. The final letters were cut out with a saw and either scanned or photographed before they were treated digitally.

activated and the mind works on hyper-mode. In terms of people that inspired us, I'd have to give it up to Robert Rauschenberg, the guys from Studio Braun and Erlend Oye.

What has been repeatedly used in your artwork?

Off-hand illustration is definitely one repeating element. We also try to work physically as much as possible – that's why we're always building things – fonts or installations. I'd say 44flavours is about the "human touch". And then there's also the mysterious 44flavours' dog, who follows us everywhere we go.

What does your work teach you?

In terms of craft, we're always improving our techniques and learning or developing new ones. In terms of client relations – the power of intuition and adaptability are probably the biggest lessons – that and Zen like patience.

Who is the No.1 leading-edge designer in your mind? Ask him/her a question.

The past couple of years we've been digging some French designers: M/M from Paris and LeClubDesChevreuils, their

What is the wildest/craziest design practice you have done over the years?

We work a lot with hand-made typography – we basically build our fonts out of all types of materials, found objects, etc. Recently we're really into wood! We love the aged

Please describe a moment/thing/person that has a strong influence on your work.

Time is a strong influence. If we have a lot of it on our hands we daydream ourselves into new ideas. And when we're crunching to meet deadlines that extra sense gets

work is solid and we're definitely feeling their spirit! Apart from that we have to big up some of our friends like the cats from KLUB7 and KINGDRIPS as well as the artist Philipp Dorl, the forward thinking designers Tim Rehm and Tim Sürken and last but not least we have to mention our colleagues at Trapped In Suburbia from The Hague, who realized some amazing events in the past two years. They are all very special in their fields.

And the question is: Can you recommend a fresh movie that I could watch tonight?

What makes you say "wooow!!" lately?

The latest album by The Roots, the exhibitions "Welt aus Schrift" and "Schrift als Bild" at Kulturforum in Berlin. Funny van Dannen and of course Julio's little nephew Miró, who can play drums like he's rocking with Slayer and he's only 3!

What's the most important to you now?

Apart from our families, girlfriends and friends...to be able to live and work in a peaceful and open minded surrounding. To take the time and just relax, to have the time to read books, to play soccer, to travel, to cook soul food and build. — To enjoy life! Now? Thinking of the summer in Berlin already - ping pong sessions at lunch time every day :)

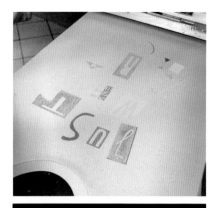

PHENÜM
Typography/Illustration
2010

" *Time is a strong influence. If we have a lot of it on our hands we daydream ourselves into new ideas. And when we're crunching to meet deadlines that extra sense gets activated and the mind works on hyper-mode.* "

No Guarantee
Exhibition
2008

Robot Koch -
Listen to Them Fade
Packaging/Typography/Illustration
2010

Created in 2006 in Lyon and now in Paris, "A is a name" is a studio for multidisciplinary graphic design, managed by two artistic directors who graduated from the department of visual communication of the Ecole Superieur des Arts Decoratif in Strasbourg. The studio has developed a great variety of artistic projects for a broad range of institutions, such as -rms and associations and, in parallel, also provides custom-designed projects.

A is a Name

Big
Dish Go 5th
Birthday Party 2
presents

Ivan
Smagghe

(Kill the DJ / It's a Fine Line)

&

Andrew Weaterall

(Rotters Golf Club)

5 Hours Back to Back Set
Friday March
4th

The
Underground
@ Kennedys,
Westland Row, D.2

Doors 10pm

Admission €15 before 11.30pm / €20 after
Limited early bird tickets
€10 / Pre Sale €15

Tickets available from:
www.eventelephant.
com/5thbdayparty2

afewthingsfromi-
vansmagghe.
blogspot.
com

A FEW THINGS FROM...

How did you get the name "A is a Name"?

This name came to us when we rebuilt our website. We wanted to be more precise about our design project and we needed a name, which we wanted to be even more related to the international area. We believe that everything (in graphic design) is related to the typography, that's the only thing that we will never question in our process, and the capital A is a kind of icon that condenses this idea. So it's looked like a mathematical equation, A = an every thing. We are constantly playing with that: A is a name, A is a rounded square, A is a god...

What is the wildest/craziest design practice you have done over the years?

For the project called "The A from Outer Space", we needed to shoot pictures around our location (that was Lyon in France at this time) and we wanted a place that looks like an outer space planet. We found a desert place close to a military base, we knew it but we thought the place was empty, and we used a smoke grenade! So the military police came, and we had to stop but they actually laughed a lot, because it was the first time they arrested two dumb guys like us.

A Few Things from
Ivan Smagghe
Poster
2011

Please describe a moment/stuff/person that has a strong influence on your work.

Stefan Sagmeister is a strong influence, not because of his work but the way that he thinks.

We like the way that he never does the same work two times.

What has been repeatedly used in your artwork?

Typography. Question every time. Be precise. The core issue. Attention to detail. Playfulness.

What does your work teach you?
Precision and now we know that details matter.

Who is the No.1 leading-edge designer in your mind? Ask him/her a question.

Stefan Sagmeister. - "May I work for you? Please..."

What's the most important to you now?
Books & Music.

The A from Outer Space
Self-initiated
2009

May 2010 / Identity / Music Label

MARKETING
MARKETING
MARKETING

AAABCDEEFGGG
HIJJKKKLMMMNMW
OPQRRRSTTTU
VWXYZ

£¶&:;?!()
0123456789
0123456789

A LABEL FOR
CONTEMPORARY
MUSIC

BRAWNY GODS
JUST FLOCKED UP
TO QUIZ
AND VEX HIM

May 2010 / Custom Typography / Music Label

Marketing Music
Identity/Custom typeface
2010

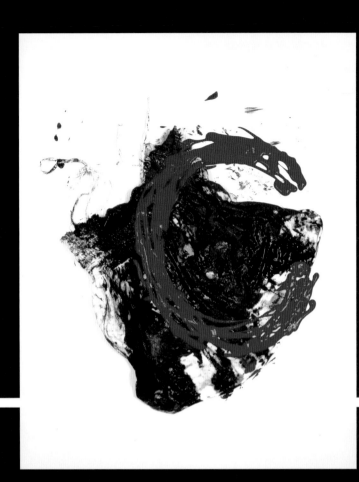

Magali Jeambrun
Furniture design
2010
Art direction and
photography with Véronique
Pêcheux

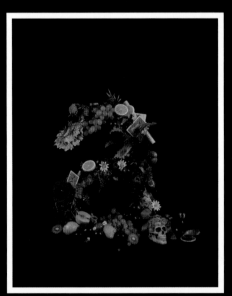

UNIVERSE OSCILLATION > 06/04/11 > 20/04/11 > VERNISSAGE > 06/04/11 > 19:00
A IS A NAME
WWW.AIS-A.NAME

LA GALERIE TOUTOUCHIC
WWW.LETOUTOUCHIC.COM

aakkforever is a small product and graphic design studio of two members - Adam Turecek (36-year-old) & Kristina Ambrozova (30-year-old) established at AAAD - Academy of Art, Architecture and Design, Prague, where they began study in 2008. The major part of their work is commercial, but they still work on their own projects like Do-it-yourself.cz and non-profit projects. They are always looking for new ways to combine vision and practice.

aakkforever

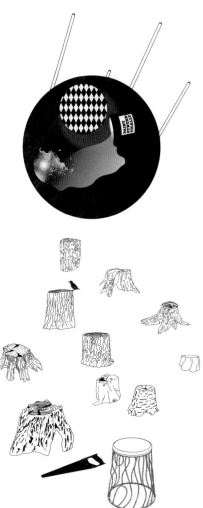

Album of Peto Tazok &
Karaoke Tundra
Packaging/Illustration
2010
Design: Adam

CTRLC (Self-initiated)
Website/Art direction/Illustration/
Packaging/Video
2007
Design: Adam

What's your typical day look like?

A: Alarm at 7am/ Organic coffee/ Walk our dog – named Pupik/ Check Email – all day/ Work/ Organic lunch or walk our dog/ Work/ Walk our dog/ Organic dinner/ Work or movie/ Sleep/ Walk our dog/ Sleep.

K: Alarm at 8am/ Alarm at 8:10am/ Alarm at 8:15am/ Alarm at 8:20am.../ Green tea/ Breakfast/ Walk our dog/ Work/ Organic lunch or walk our dog/ Work/ Walk our dog/ Organic dinner/ Work or movie/ Sleep.

What is the wildest/craziest design practice you have done over the years?

K: Masters Hammer Fun club, because I have to learn heavy metal.

A: CTRL C – my own music project. I made a song for the first time.

Please describe a moment/thing/person that has a strong influence on your work.

K: Beginning studies at AAAD.

A: When I met Arik Levy at Vitra Summer Workshop.

What has been repeatedly used in your artwork?

K: Type Nudista of Suitcase Type Foundry and Bodoni; Women's legs.

A: I sample my unused work and ideas; My brain; Robots, because I love them.

What does your work teach you?

K: More thinking and more drawing.

A: Not all work will be paid.

Who is the No.1 leading-edge designer in your mind? Ask him/her a question.

A&K: Štěpán Malovec from designair.eu absolutely.

- "When did you get married?"

What makes you say "wooow!!" lately?

A: Quayola's project – Strata #3.

What's the most important to you now?

K: Our own new apartment/ Final examination on AAAD / Graphic design and illustration for project Cookbook – a seasonal Czech cook book I prepared with my friends Iva Jakesova – chef and Marek Bartos – photographer.

A: Our own new apartment/ Upcoming work on the do-it-yourself.cz project – it's about free CC the licensed furniture and etc. designed by us.

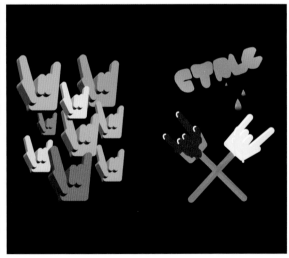

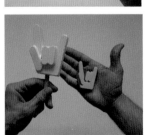

Vibrator
Posters for Vibrator
music party in Club
Roxy Prague
2010
Design: Kristina

THE ARCADE FIRE

Arcade fire event
Illustration/Concept
2008
Design: Kristina

" *I sample my unused work and ideas;*
My brain; Robots, because I love them. "

Designsupermarket -
Prague Design Festival
Website/Art direction/
Illustration/Posters/Flyers/
TV Spot
2009
Design: Kristina

A graphic design studio that focuses on turning every project into a true visual story, the personal story of the client. Their work deeply explore the font, the color, the paper and the look. The devil is in the detail.

Their clients range from small exclusive goldsmith and architecture company to the National Army Museum and large health care centers.

All the Way to Paris

Sing Tehus
Art direction/Illustration/
Packaging
2010

Why call the studio "All the Way to Paris"?

We took the name as we wanted a name that creates associations and evokes the imagination in people. It also works as a reminder of how it is important in good design to go all the way...

Tanja, if Elin were a smell, what would it be?

The smell of macciato and an exquisite Darjeeling tea.

Petra, if Tanja were a shape, what would it be?

The shape of roughly cut diamond.

Elin, if Matilde were a sound, what would it be?

The sound of a string quartet.

Matilde, if Petra were a color, what would it be?

A dark emerald green.

What is the wildest/craziest design practice you have done over the years?

It's been great to work with the artist Jeppe Hein and his travelling CIRCUS HEIN. Making the Circus Hein newspaper in the old ever so used broadsheet-format might not have been wild and crazy, but very

exciting and fulfilling for us as graphic designers.

What has been repeatedly used in your artwork?

Every project starts with a common brainstorm ending with a couple of concepts – then very open sketches on the wall – another conceptual brainstorm and then the discussion is narrowed down. This process is repeated in all of our projects.

Please describe a moment/thing/person that has a strong influence on your work.

Meeting new and old clients always influences us as they are all very diverse and in that challenge us to do our very best/most of our work.

What does your work teach you?

That a good dialogue and communication with your client is everything.

Who is the No.1 leading-edge designer in your mind? Ask him/her a question.

The world is full of talented and interesting designers – each interesting in its own way. But if we were to choose two it would be Charles and Ray Eames.

The question would be: Would you please come and have tea with us?

Circus Hein
VI/Poster/Editorial/Art
direction/Illustration/
Exhibition/Website
2009

What makes you say "wooow!!" lately?

The urban life outside our studio window in the very center of Copenhagen. People from all of the world, the Danish queen, wave-boarders, political demonstrations, musicians – looking out our window anything can happen.

What's the most important to you now?

Challenge, dialogue and JOY.

Rebekka Notkin
VI/ Art direction/Illustration/
Packaging/Website
2009

*" A good dialogue and communication
with your client is everything. "*

Geist
VI/ Art direction/Illustration/
Website
2011

BACKSTAGE 2 /
NO SMOKING /
WI-FI: PUMPNET
ACCESS CODE:
ab16061606

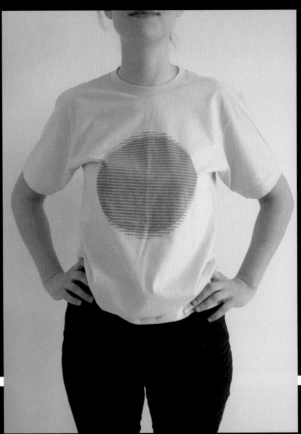

1 MINUTE/
ET MINUT
ER OVER DEM
ALLE

8 SULTNE FREESTYLERAPPERE /
1 MINUTE MEN / SPECTORS / WHITE PONY /
+ SPECIAL GUESTS

Pumpehuset
VI/Poster/Art
direction/Website
2009

Pumpehuset Rabal
Børnekultur
VI/ Art direction/Poster/
Illustration/Website
2010

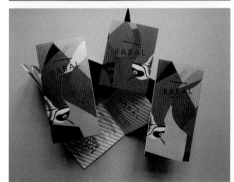

Angus
MacPherson

**Young Typographic
Designers (YTD)**
Identity
2010

Angus MacPherson has just graduated from Leeds College of Art with a First Class Degree in BA (Hons) Graphic Design. He's excited about typography, publications and beautiful print finishes and he is currently looking for full-time work or placement opportunities. Outside of design he's into riding BMX and taking photos.

What's your favorite part of your day?

Getting up after a good night's sleep, the first sip of coffee always tastes amazing! Or just after a good day's work and you get to see your friends and tell them about the day.

What is the wildest/craziest design practice you have done over the years?

I seemed to spend a lot of my first year at university experimenting with weird practices for different projects. Like writing long convoluted questionnaires to try and encourage people to vote, collecting huge amounts of research data for an information design project about my friends, collecting bike tire skid marks to create an image or getting covered in spray paint making posters.

Please describe a moment/ thing/person that has a strong influence on your work.

I think my tutor, Fred, at university was a really big influence. He gave me the ethic to work really, really hard to try and create something that is the absolute best you can possibly do. Also people like Paula Sher who just go on creating really original and exciting design work for years and years inspire me. Never allowing yourself to get comfortable and always pushing yourself to do new things is something I strive for.

Aside from that I think I am quite influenced by looking at design history and design from years ago that people have forgotten about or overlooked, I think that would be one of my biggest influences.

What has been repeatedly used in your artwork?

I think that the things that I always come back to with my work are typography and craft. I would say that typography is usually one of the first things I consider when I start on a new project and more often than not it is at the very

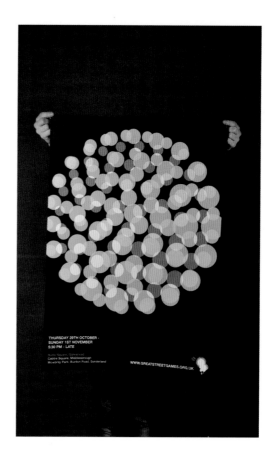

Great Street Games
Logo/Poster
2009

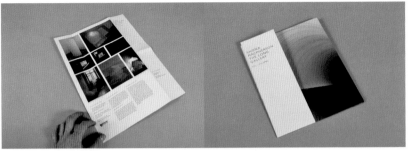

Shona MacPherson
Identity
2010

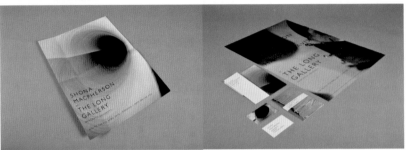

center of the solution to the project. Personally for me craft is very important, it can only take a few seconds to come up with a good idea but to get that idea resolved and produced to the very best of your ability can often take weeks and weeks. I like to think that all my work has a strong element of craft in it, whether it's the print and finish of the product or the endless attention to detail in a typeface I like to try and craft everything really well.

What does your work teach you?

You can do anything you put your mind to.

"You can do anything you put your mind to."

Who is the No.1 leading-edge designer in your mind? Ask him/her a question.

This is really difficult because there are so many ridiculous designers out there. I'd ask Michael C Place whether he has ever worked more than 24 hours non-stop? I get the impression he works really, really hard!

What makes you say "wooow!!" lately?

It's nothing to do with design but I recently went cycling in the Cévennes Mountains in France and one day we descended from 1300 meters to near sea level over about 3 hours on newly tarmaced roads, I couldn't think of anything that has put a bigger smile on my face recently!

In terms of design the Neon Noise Project posters by ISO really blew me away, along with a lot of other work they have done.

What's the most important to you now?

It's not very original but it's my family and friends, they are the ones who keep me sane and cheer me up when I'm sad.

Also I suppose trying to have fun with graphic design and trying to get somewhere with it.

UP
DOWN
LEFT
RIGHT
CAN
CAN'T
IN
OUT
DON'T
KNOW!

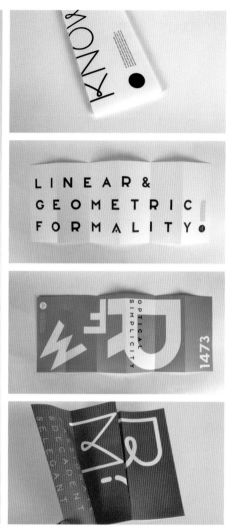

Type Specimen
School project
2010

No Format Font & Identity
Typography/Identity
2011

Ashlea O'Neill is a freelance designer originally from Australia and now based in London. Her work ranges from conceptual design through to art direction over various disciplines including print, packaging and web.

Ashlea O'Neill

What's your favorite part of your day?

Definitely the morning. Porridge, news, a walk to work. Best time for fresh ideas.

What is the wildest/ craziest design practice you have done over the years?

I covered a whole room and person in sticky notes, that was perhaps not wild but crazy for the amount of time it took.

Please describe a moment/thing/person that has a strong influence on your work.

Combinations of the above – definitely. Designers better than me constantly push me as well as all the little aspects of my environment. Sometimes you can be so surprised and influenced by the smallest details you neglected to see every other day.

What has been repeatedly used in your artwork?

I'm not going to lie – I love circles...however thinking back – I keep them pretty restrained.

What does your work teach you?

PATIENCE!!!!!

Monster & Midget Magazine
Print/Editorial design/Identity
2009 - Current
Collaboration with Thembi Hanify

MONSTER &
MIDGET

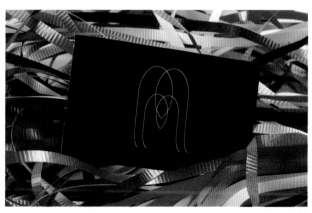

Who is the No.1 leading-edge designer in your mind? Ask him/her a question.

My number one designer is David Band, Melbourne. As an artist too his work is truly beautiful. I guess I'd ask him – where does it come from?

What makes you say "wooow!!" lately?

The fact that it's sunny and warm in London today!

What's the most important to you now?

At the risk of sounding like a dork – becoming really good and enjoying the youthfulness of design.

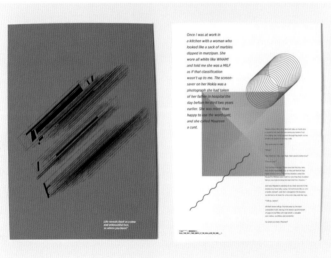

"Patience!!!!!"

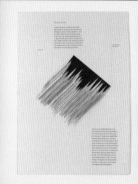

Monster & Midget Magazine
Print/Editorial design/Identity
2009 - Current
Collaboration with Thembi Hanify

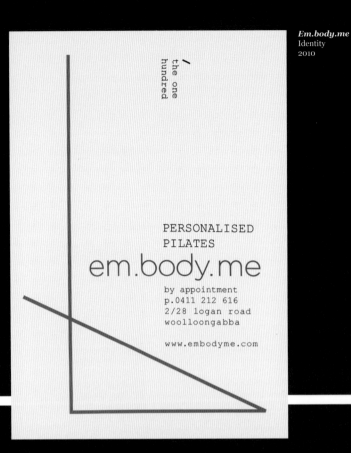

Em.body.me
Identity
2010

Merry Christmas Card
Typography
2010

dear you

This is an impression of what your A5 card, which *may* have been printed on a nice matt stock *could* have looked like *if* I were one of those people who took down addresses and had the initiative to make the brave step to the post office. But seeing you are all my friends—you know i am far from being that person. My emails are as scarce as the sunshine in London...and that's even if you've been lucky to see a few of my literary rays. BUT my friends & lovers—the reason you get this email is that you know i am a gansta rapper. And you know that sometimes it's hard out there for a pimp—managing personalised correspondence along with my 16crt diamond encrusted bling. Though in all seriousness, the point of this little ramble was to wish you all a very safe and jolly festive season full of sunshine, warmth, sweat, and humidity. I'll be thinking of and missing you all as my padded body does its penguin waddle across the SNOW in search for the christmas squirrel. Flip side home dogs, I'll be sniffing your tree trunk soon. Squirrel!? Love as always—your dickhead forever, *Ashlea Valda.*

Jan Murphy Posters
Typography
2009

Brian Condron
Catalogue
Print design
2010

ESCAPE X KULTE
Collective exhibition/
Art direction
2009

Aurélien Arnaud
(PNTS studio)

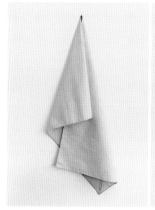

Aurélien Arnaud is a graphic designer and art director based in Lyon (France).

He founded PNTS studio with Denis Carrier in 2009.

He works all around vectorial illustration, collage and type design, and has strong interest in searches and graphic experimentations.

ESCAPE

UNE EXPOSITION COLLECTIVE DE
BASTARDGRAPHICS x SPKO x PNTS STUDIO

Exposition du 18 mars au 18 juillet 2010

**VERNISSAGE LE 17 MARS 2010
À PARTIR DE 19H**

En poussant plus loin la collaboration commencée à Lyon l'an dernier avec **Kulte**, Bastardgraphics, SPKO et le studio PNTS sont à nouveau réunis pour présenter leur travail, autour de la nouvelle collection *THE ESCAPE*.
Les quatre artistes vous proposent un exode sensible et graphique autour de l'évasion, du voyage, des rêves et de toutes sortes d'autres échappatoires.

BOUTIQUE KULTE - 76, RUE VIEILLE DU TEMPLE - PARIS

K kulte.   **PNTS**

ESCAPE

UNE EXPOSITION COLLECTIVE DE
BASTARDGRAPHICS x SPKO x PNTS STUDIO

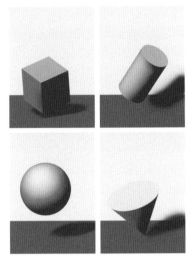  

Semi Permanent
Illustration
2010

Standard Magazine
Editorial illustration
2010

Equilibria x Sehubabe
Tee-shirt illustration
2011

Decibelles
CD cover/Art direction
2010

What does your typical day look like?

I wake up at 8am. I ride my bike to the studio and work from 9 til 1pm. Then I have a quick lunch at home; it lasts 1- 2 hours usually. After that I use digesting time wisely to do some graphic research. Around 7pm I leave the office and play music all night long.

What is the wildest/craziest design practice you have done over the years?

We created new designs for gloves; it was really new to work on that kind of product. We also designed a flag for the collective exhibition Escape in Paris, along with Kulte (French apparel brand). It was very interesting to work with a street wear designer.

Please describe a moment/thing/person that has a strong influence on your work.

It's very important for me to have some breaks during the year. I love to travel and meet people. I like to discover how the graphic culture and mentalities evolve in other cities and countries. Being a freelance graphic designer, it's important to have holidays far from the office. When I come back, I feel better, and I'm very excited. A lot of inspiration comes then.

What has been repeatedly used in your artwork?

At the moment, I work a lot with collages. I have to search for pictures on the internet to create samples. This is something I do everyday, all the time. I mainly work around graphic disturbance, and I find that the link between graphic design and my illustration production is very important.

la Fleche d'Or
Poster/Illustration
2010

What does your work teach you?

Again, again and again.

Who is the No.1 leading-edge designer in your mind? Ask him/her a question.

Antoine et Manuel – "Guys, c'mon! What's wrong with you??"
This is exactly what I love: graphic design + illustration + experimentation.

What makes you say "wooow!!" lately?

The Sacred Mtn's portfolio and a Lithuanian girl.

What's the most important to you now?

To meet and work with interesting people, to experiment with new techniques, to feel new, to travel still far away and produce new stuff everyday.

Benthos Phona
Art direction
2009/2010

Cruel Summer
Art direction
2010

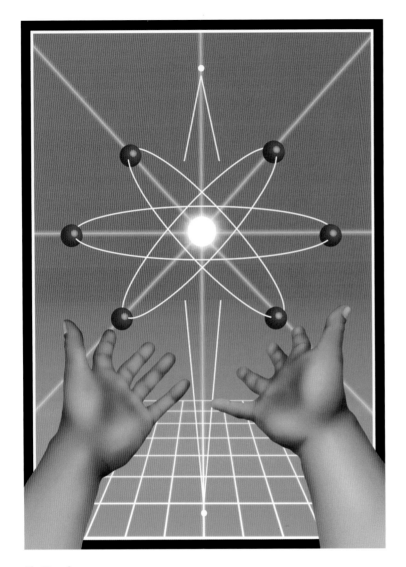

"To meet and work with interesting people, to experiment with new techniques, to feel new, to travel still far away and produce new stuff everyday."

**The Star of
Bethnal Green**
Poster/Illustration
2010

L'ÉCOLE TECHNIQUE DES ARTS APPLIQUÉS DE GRENOBLE, ETAAG.

L'École Technique des Arts Appliqués de Grenoble est un établissement supérieur privé ayant pour objectif de former des créateurs dans le domaine des Arts Appliqués. À travers notre enseignement, nos moyens pédagogiques et nos partenaires professionnels, nous vous orientons vers l'acquisition de solides compétences vous permettant d'exercer dans la sphère artistique.
La pédagogie est au cœur des préoccupations de notre Établissement.

L'ETAAG est une école à taille humaine où chaque élève fait l'objet d'un suivi individualisé par une équipe pédagogique disponible, compétente et à l'écoute.
L'ETAAG vous accompagne tout au long de votre cursus à la définition et à la formalisation de votre projet professionnel, au développement de votre potentiel, à la construction de votre avenir professionnel.

Cyril VASSEL
Responsable de la filière

MISE À NIVEAU DES ARTS APPLIQUÉS (MANAA)

Assurer un juste équilibre entre réflexion et pratique.
L'année de mise à niveau des Arts Appliqués aide l'étudiant à se positionner dans le domaine artistique.
Cette formation d'un an est obligatoire pour tout titulaire d'un bac général souhaitant intégrer un BTS (brevet de technicien supérieur) d'arts appliqués.

Alliant enseignements généraux et artistiques, la MANAA constitue une véritable année laboratoire. Elle a pour objectif d'assurer une mise à niveau d'ordre artistique par des apprentissages spécifiques d'ordre culturelle, théoriques et pratiques.
Offrant la possibilité de conforter l'étudiant dans son choix d'orientation, l'apprentissage repose sur l'acquisition d'outils et de moyens techniques appliqués à des réalisations commanditées par un chef de projet. Curiosité, ouverture et culture s'adjoindront à une pratique quotidienne et rigoureuse des bases graphiques.

CLASSE PRÉPARATOIRE

Développer des compétences dans les domaines artistiques. Cette classe préparatoire, volontairement généraliste, est une formation d'un an permettant d'acquérir une maitrise des modes d'expression plastique en vue d'une préparation aux concours des écoles d'art les plus réputées (Art déco, Beaux-arts). Ces formations artistiques, accessibles uniquement sur concours, requièrent une importante ouverture culturelle et de solides connaissances aux différentes pratiques artistiques.

Au cours de cette année les élèves pourront mesurer leur degré d'implication et de motivation dans cet objectif d'orientation artistique.

Son programme, s'articule autour d'apprentissages pratiques (photo, graphisme, expression plastique...) et théoriques dans la perspective de constitution d'un dossier de travaux personnels.

La réussite de l'élève repose sur l'acquisition de moyens d'expression et de réflexion ainsi que de son engagement dans une démarche Artistique.

BTS COMMUNICATION VISUELLE

Coordonner la conception et l'articulation de messages visuels. Cette formation sanctionnée par un diplôme d'état, est axée sur la compréhension et la maitrise des différentes techniques et des divers supports de communication.
La prise en considération des besoins et des contraintes définis dans la commande client, constitue les fondements de cet apprentissage.
Le technicien en communication visuelle adoptera un état d'esprit autant créatif que rigoureux.

GRAPHISME
ÉDITION
PUBLICITÉ

BTS DESIGN D'ESPACE

Interagir dans la conception des espaces privés et publics.
Ce diplôme d'état s'appuie sur les différentes échelles de l'espace : de la conception de mobilier à l'aménagement d'un espace.

L'approche pluridisciplinaire offre à l'étudiant la possibilité d'élargir sa culture générale, artistique et technique. En phase avec l'actualité, une large ouverture d'esprit sera nécessaire pour s'ouvrir aux conceptions nouvelles d'une société en pleine mutation.

L'ensemble des matières générales, plastiques, et professionnelles concourent à la prise de conscience des contraintes éthiques, économiques, législatives et esthétiques inhérentes aux métiers de Designer d'Espace.

ÉCOLE
TECHNIQUE
D'ARTS
APPLIQUÉS
DE GRENOBLE

21, RUE TURENNE   T. 04 76 46 92 41   SCOLAIRE & ALTERNANCE
38000 GRENOBLE   F. 04 76 47 01 10   WWW.ETAAG.FR

Remerciements aux étudiants de la filière d'Arts Appliqués (promotion 2008-2009) pour leurs travaux

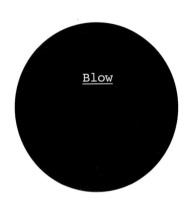

Blow

Backroom Conversations
VI
2010

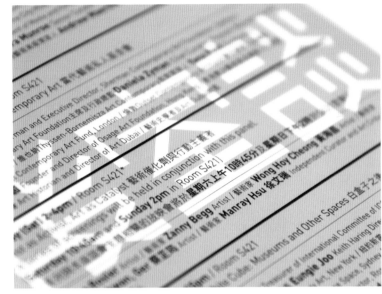

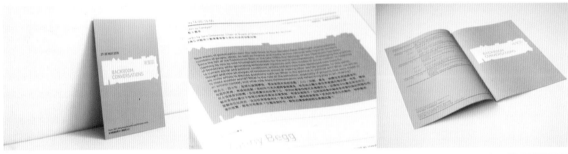

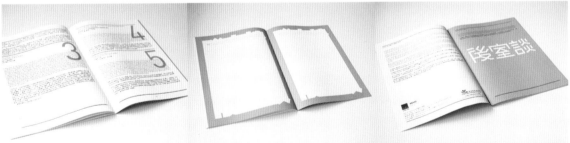

Born in Hong Kong, Ken graduated from HKU SPACE Community College with Distinction in a Higher Diploma in Visual Communication in 2005. He joined Alan Chan Design Company in 2006 and became a Senior Designer in 2007.

After leaving Alan Chan Design Company in 2010, Ken set up his own design company, BLOW, and launched his tote bag brand, luckipocki, aiming to spread positive messages and share good luck with everyone around the world.

What does your typical day look like?

Working over 12 hours, sleeping less than 6 hours.

What is the wildest/craziest design practice you have done over the years?

This year I have launched my tote bag brand – luckipocki. I prepared this project for a whole year. As I have a job in the daytime, I can only work on this project after work. However, I found this project is quite hard to do, because I am the designer as well as the client. I always try to avoid being too personal on the direction. Besides the design development part, I also needed to coordinate with the manufacturer. In order to complete this project, finally I had to quit my day job. I think this is the wildest design practice and decision I have made during the past few years.

Please describe a moment/thing/person that has a strong influence on your work.

Codesign was the first working place in my career. I worked there when I was a design student. Eddy Yu and Hung Lam taught me many things about design details. I still remember how they keep refining the design until the last minute!

Creative Underground
CI
2009

Although the process is quite tough, I have trained my design execution and attitude. After leaving Codesign, I joined Alan Chan Design Company. During the time I worked there, Alan Chan reminded me a lot about technique in doing commercial jobs and presentation. This really helps me to communicate with my clients efficiently.

What has been repeatedly used in your artwork?

A clear idea with a simple and bold style.

What does your work teach you?

A successful design doesn't only depend on the designer; we also need a good client to work with. If the client didn't cooperate with you, sometimes the outcome could be a disaster.

Who is the No.1 leading-edge designer in your mind? Ask him/her a question.

Kashiwa Sato.
How can he always go picnic with his family, while his workload is so heavy?

Luckipocki
Branding
2010

What makes you say "wooow!!" lately?

My 16-month old daughter, I think. She says many unexpected words recently. This always makes me happy and surprised.

What's the most important to you now?

Many things are important to me. My family, my career, my health...I always want to have a balance between them. But physically, I think the most important to me now is to take a good sleep.

ECF
VI
2008
Copywriter:
Stealla Lo

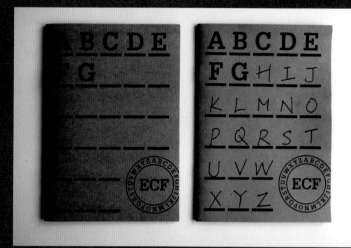

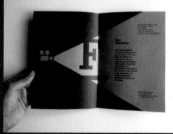

"Many things are important to me. My family, my career, my health...I always want to have a balance between them. But physically, I think the most important to me now is to take a good sleep."

Luckipocki
Branding
2010

Casper Chan is a graphic designer, illustrator and stylist currently based in London. He graduated from The Hong Kong Polytechnic University, School of Design in 2006 with a major in visual communication design.

Casper Chan's portfolio diversely synthesizes typography, illustration and fashion styling. In 2007, his final year project – "Imperfect beauty in daily life", publication was selected by FABRICA, the Benetton group communications research centre. He was awarded the British council 60th anniversary scholarship in contribution toward an MA in Graphic Design at London College of Communication in 2009. In 2011, he formed Studio 247 with Monkey Leung Man Kin in order to pursue a shared dream in graphic design and visual representation.

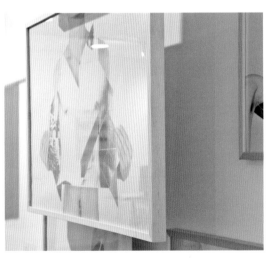

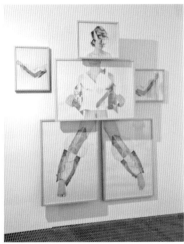

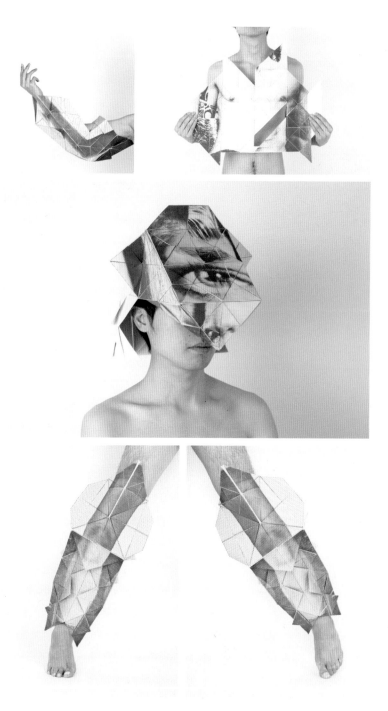

Fabricated Body
(Self-initiated)
Installation
2010

What does your typical day look like?

12:00am – 6:00am.
I enjoy the silence and solitude of that time of day. I can fully concentrate on my work without much disturbance. Sometimes, we have to separate ourselves from the crowd by isolating ourselves.
To feel the nothingness.
To cleanse our mind.
It is the best time of my day. The dawn after 6 hours of work delights my day.

What is the wildest/craziest design practice you have done over the years?

To me, the wildest thing I did was when I decided to quit my job in Hong Kong and go to London to pursue my further education. I am a very attached type of person to my family and friends and when I made up my mind to leave all these loves behind me, I got lots of questions and doubts in my mind. The feeling is like sailing in the sea but without having any maps at all. But such kind of unpredictability makes my life become a journey where I am always fascinated to discover more.

Please describe a moment/thing/person that has a strong influence on your work.

My mother.

She is not a designer or artist. However, she knows the creative industry never was an easy business. Although there are ups and downs in my creative journey, she is always the one who supports me. Also, her wisdom is inexplicably full of humor and charm. I see a beautiful woman nurturing her family at its best. So I just want to create something beautiful in return for her love. I want to express love, romanticism and passion through my works.

What has been repeatedly used in your artwork?

I like simple forms and colours and I am sure you see a lot of red used in my works.

I want my works to possess a feeling of dynamism and fluidity.

What does your work teach you?

We, as designers, are part of a group of people who are responsible for reevaluating existing norms and values. Our mission is not only to solve existing problems but also to reveal the problem itself. By expressing what we believe and anticipating counter arguments, we hope to encourage dialogue and shape a better future for people.

Who is the No.1 leading-edge designer in your mind? Ask him/her a question.

Hedi Slimane.
When was the last time you cried?

What makes you say "wooow!!" lately?

My own design studio – Studio 247 is emerging from a concept to reality. I collaborate with my fellow art director Monkey Leung to express our love for art, aesthetics and design. We still believe there is another way to show design in a less commercial and more personal way. So I cannot wait to show our first project to the public.

Human Connection
Poster
2009

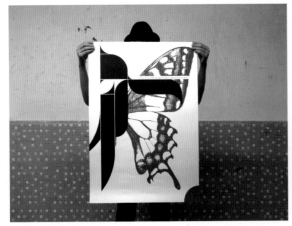

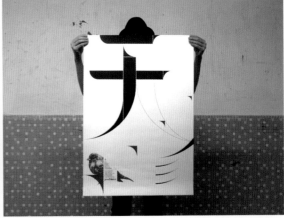

"Although there are ups and downs in my creative journey, she (my mother) is always the one who supports me. Also, her wisdom is inexplicably full of humor and charm. I see a beautiful woman nurturing her family at its best. So I just want to create something beautiful in return for her love. I want to express love, romanticism and passion through my works."

Social Etiquette
Poster
2010

Faye Wong

Mother Teresa

Stella McCartney

Ringo Shiina

Vivienne Westwood

Charlotte Gainsbourg

Cate Blanchett

Rebecca Poon

Audrey Hepburn

Jane Birkin

Madonna

Tilda Swinton

Princess Diana

Anna Wintour

bonjour!
i am topaz
leung, a free-
lance photogra-
pher, writer and
stylist from hong
kong. my website is
www.topazleung.
com and my email
address is topaz@
topazleung.com.
you can also
reach me at
+852 6033 2219.

see you.

Topaz Leung
Namecard
Visual identity
2009

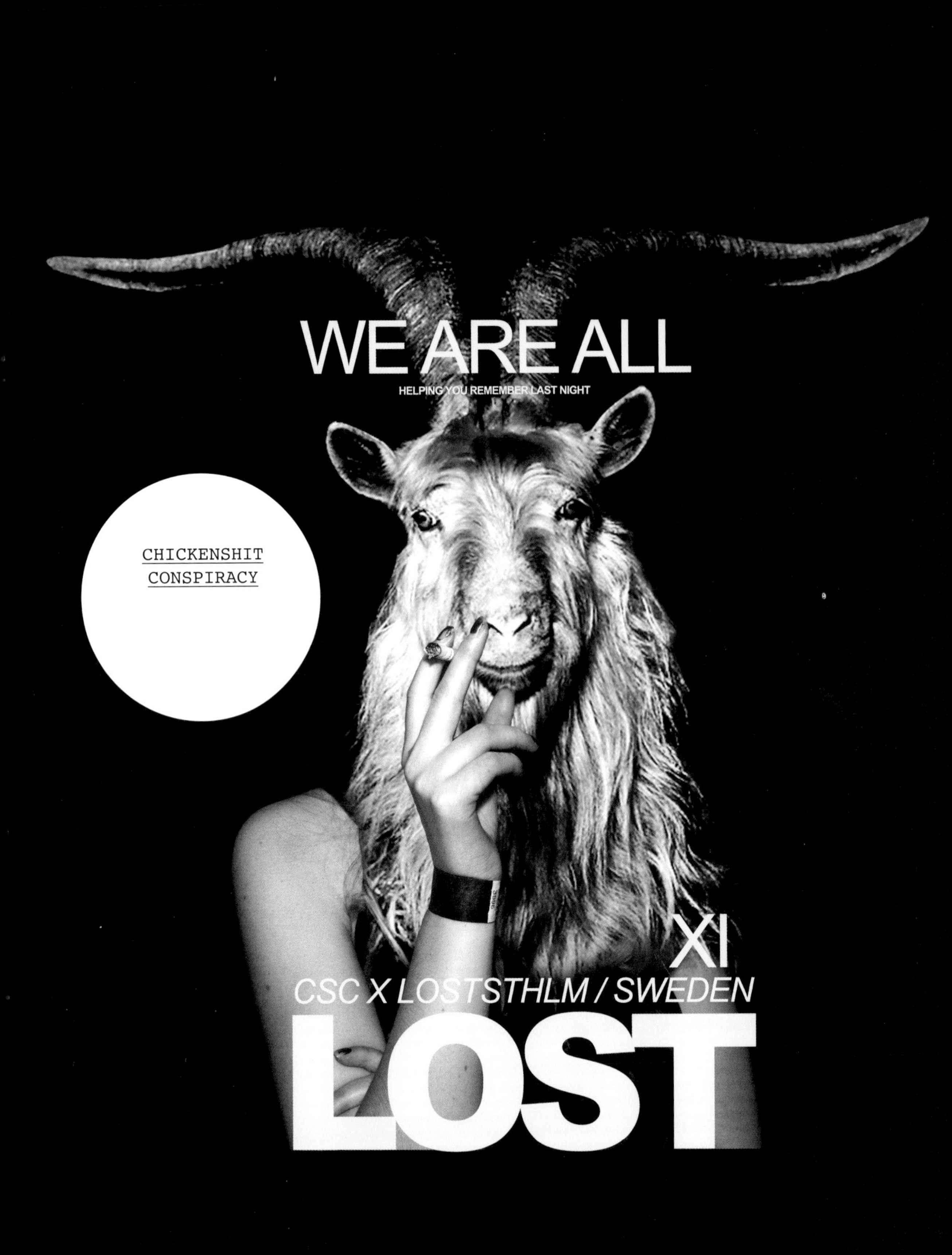

WE ARE ALL

HELPING YOU REMEMBER LAST NIGHT

CHICKENSHIT
CONSPIRACY

XI

CSC X LOSTSTHLM / SWEDEN

LOST

(Left)
CSC X loststhlm
Product/Illustration/Party
2010

(Right)
*CHICKENSHIT X
Diana Luganski*
Product
2009

CHICKENSHIT CONSPIRACY is a Russian-based creative community and a fashion brand, established by 3 designers in 2006. Originally created as a not-for-profit label, today chickenshit is available for international wholesale. Chickenshit collections are the result of the process where creative graphics, a strong concept and a dark mood are the main source of inspiration.

"You can make whatever you want and we are always proud to see people wearing our product."

How did you get the name Chickenshit?

We like how these two words, "chicken" and "shit" sound together and it is easy to remember. We make fashion shit for bad guys. In Chickenshit we use themes like outlaws, occultism, voodoo, and dark moods.

What is the wildest/craziest design practice you have done over the years?

It was when we were printing the design for the fashion show of Russian designer Leonid Alexeev. The print is the inverted cross. And we couldn't finish the print because the cross caught on fire when we tried to dry it. (The cause was the material which includes polyester). That's why we made just 5 of this item!

What has been repeatedly used in your artwork?

Knotan is our favorite photographer and we like to work and collaborate with him. He is one of the best.

What distinguishes your work from that of your contemporaries?

We pay much attention to the presentation of the product and packaging. Chickenshit is not only clothes; exhibitions, installations, performances, parties and clothes are also elements of design.

What is the best part of being a designer?

You can make whatever you want and we are always proud to see people wearing our product.

What would you like to be if you were not a designer?

Monk and Kung-fu master.

What makes you say "wooow!!" recently?

An exhibition of Knotan in Saint Petersburg - three days of preparation, 52 pictures, and more than 1250 visitors who showed up for the opening party.

SAVE your NOSSSE + MEYOKO
Product/Illustration
2010

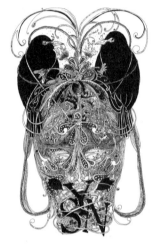

SAVE your NOSSSE + KNOTAN
Exhibition/Product
2009

CSC X loststhlm
Product/Illustration/
Party
2010

**Favourite Scandinavian
Photographer/ Knotan**
Exhibition/Product
2008

Favourite Scandinavian
Photographer / Knotan
Exhibition/Product
2008

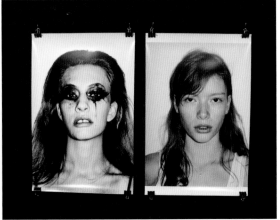

Spectacle by
Karl Grandin
Exhibition/Product
2011

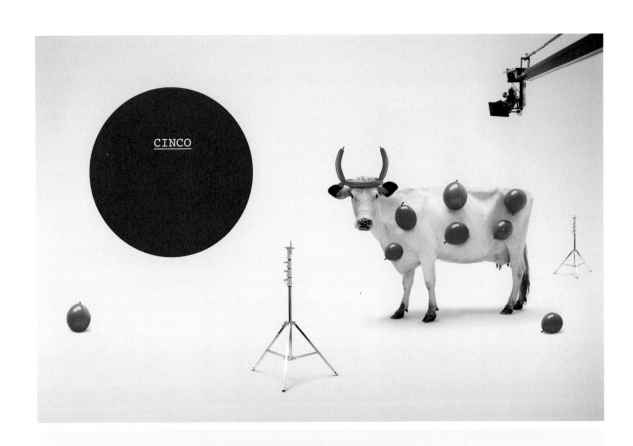

CINCO

Red Creek
Poster
2008
Photography: Urko Suaya

How did you get the name CINCO?

That is not an easy question for us to answer. In spite of our name, "five" in Spanish, we are three partners, this is our first incongruity. The name came up when we hadn't even thought of the studio. The two of us, Loly Carnero and Mariano Sigal started talking about a space where all our creative interests would meet. The name symbolically includes plenty of meanings and they are all positive which is quite good. We like to manage within a small structure which prioritizes quality of work rather than quantity. At a certain point we thought about "cinco" because we would never be more than that, so you know, there are three open positions, if you happen to run into Stefan Sagmeister, Spike Jonze and Michel Gondry1 please have them send their resumes to us at toto@nosotroscinco. com

What is the wildest/craziest design practice you have done over the years?

Our wildest/craziest design practice was probably an article that we made for ATYPICA magazine. We had to represent "the future" so we developed a kind of ironic and sarcastic representation of the human body. We used fluorescent tubes which conveyed a quite futurist sensation but are also quite bizarre and retro. We took a walk through the streets of Buenos Aires to see people's reaction while we took pictures of it. Anyway, the craziest thing was that we took care of the electronics ourselves and we actually don't know much about safety in electronics. This means that we could have lost one of our partners and we would now be called "Uno" (one) instead of "Cinco".

What has been repeatedly used in your artwork?

The pattern that we repeatedly find in our work is an ironic look over the overload of information and design sophistication for no reason. We like to handle a clear, clean and sometimes even clumsy language.

We are attracted to imperfection. We love to acknowledge we are human beings and we rather find beauty within our own limitations. Not being pretentious is our goal.

What distinguishes your work from that of your contemporaries?

Mmm...Maybe somebody observing from the outside would better answer this question, but we think that each designer, artist, photographer, illustrator, etc. has his own point of view about what he does, and a personal look. So we respect and try to have free time to find ourselves as persons (though it might sound taken from a self-help book, it is true). We try to find our deepest desires, the most heartfelt things we would like to change - and this is the best tool to shape our own look which distinguished us from the rest.

Born in Buenos Aires, Argentina, in March 2009, CINCO is a group of talented professionals in different disciplines: film, photography, graphic design, illustration and modern arts, in which everyone contributes with his/her knowledge. By the hand of Mariano Sigal and Loly Carnero, the utopia of the "imperfectly perfect work" is materialized in a new creative language composed of the personal print of each of CINCO's protagonists.

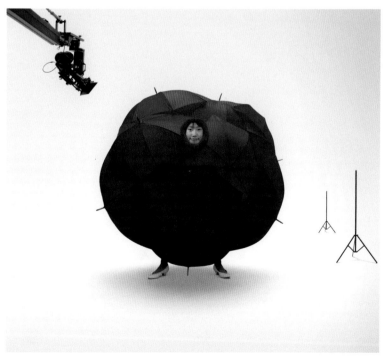

Olympicus
Poster
2009

A leading-edge designer in your mind? Ask him/her a question.

From our humble place, what can we do to change the world?

What is the best part of being a designer?

The best part of being designers for us is to have been able to come up with a place with our own language, a world where we can express ourselves in an optimistic, sarcastic, ironic or sad way, but always according to our own rules.

What would you like to be if you were not a designer?

Each of us will answer for himself/herself:
Mariano: Movie actor, I would have specially fancied to act in BMX Bandits.
Loly: I humbly consider myself a bit of a pastrycook.

What makes you say "wooow!!" lately?

We could say that to see something that we have never seen before would make us say "wooow" but we wouldn't be discovering anything new by that. Nowadays, there is so much information of every sort, in design, architecture, movies, music, photography, art, etc...We are greatly surprised when we can slow down a bit and get enthusiastic about the simple things in life such as a chat with a friend, a walk in the park, or reading without hurries. When we can achieve this, we say wooow!

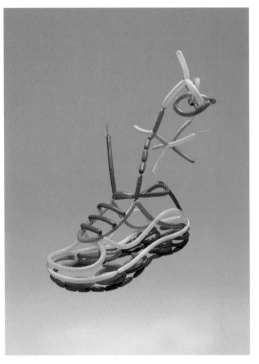

(Left)
Chori
Photography
2009

(Right)
A POM-POM
Exhibition
2009

*"We are greatly
surprised when
we can slow
down a bit and
get enthusiastic
about the simple
things in life such
as a chat with
a friend, a walk
in the park, or
reading without
hurries. When we
can achieve this,
we say wooow!"*

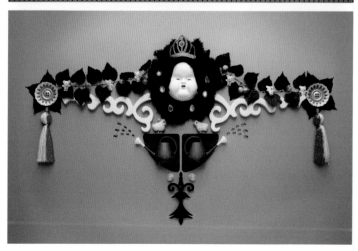

Corriette
Schoenaerts

Above the Couds
Advertising
2009

Corriette Schoenaerts's work is situated in the grey zone between art, fashion and commercial photography. She refuses to draw distinct borders between these disciplines. She also refuses to adopt a certain style, because this permits her to focus more on the subject matter of the photograph itself. She studied at the Rietveld Academy in Amsterdam (NL) and at the St-Lukas Academy in Brussels (B).

Quicker
Advertising
2009

Qualities Needed
Editorial
2007

What has been repeatedly used in your artwork?

I like to build things. It's a slow way of making that mental picture in your head physical. As a photographer the actual making of the photo is just a split second. That is just too fast for me!

What distinguishes your work from that of your contemporaries?

????? You tell me.

What is the best part of being a designer?

Being able to just go sit in a park on a sunny day, just like that... You just pick up a picnic somewhere and go.

What would you like to be if you were not a designer?

A dancer;
A civil engineer;
A special Fx person;
A stunt woman;
A furniture maker;
A good daughter;
A truck driver;
A combat pilot;
A bass player in a world famous band;
An astronaut;
A one person circus act;
A captain on a luxury yacht;
A professional rock climber;
A car mechanic;
A helicopter designer;
A chandelier collector (antiques);
A world famous chocolatier.

What makes you say "wooow!!" lately?

Adam Ondra climbed Golpe de Estado in Siurana, Spain. I am passionate about rock climbing, and that just sets the bar! Another thing that makes me happy is Favela Painting. Dre and Jeroen just rock!! For all you millionaires out there, they need more money to make their art happen!

Corriette, what does your typical day look like?

Honestly, I couldn't tell. There is no typical day, really.

What is the wildest/craziest design practice you have done over the years?

The wildest thing I've done would be the cover for FOAM Album 07.

I decided to print out all the photos that were going to be published in the book and literally cut through them, one by one. 800-something photos – all by hand...

So, the first day, I got a sore finger. The second day, I called an extra assistant and got a painful arm. The third day, I called another assistant and got a sore back and stiff neck. The fourth day, the assistant called her boyfriend for help and I was brain dead from performing the same thing over and over again...the fifth day, we were all having fits and acting like retards.

It's the only project that I've ever wanted to cancel midway, but couldn't, because I made it during Christmas holidays, so everybody was gone. Things had to go to print on Jan 2nd, so I had no choice, but to finish the whole damn thing...

"*I like to build things. It's a slow way of making that mental picture in your head physical.*"

Olympicus
Poster/Photography
2004

Daydream Nation is a Fashion Arts House founded in 2006. Aside from being an international fashion label, Daydream Nation is celebrated for its cross-disciplinary collaborations with other art forms including theatre, dance, music, film and visual arts. With the opening of its flagship store in October 2010, Daydream Nation is set to become Hong Kong's new creative hub. Alongside its own collection of clothing and accessories, it features the work of local artists and indie bands, and runs a program of creative workshops, events and happenings.

"We really believe that a dream you dream alone stays a dream; a dream you dream together is reality. We don't want this to just be about Jing and Kay; we want to create a 'United Kingdom of dreamers and lovers'."

Daydream
Nation

What does your typical day look like?

Kay: My typical day consists of emails, invoicing, talking to customers on the phone, planning work for the team, working on design planning and handwork, sourcing fabrics in Sham Shui Po, communicating with our in-house production team, daydreaming when I find the time, doing interviews with magazines occasionally...

Jing: My typical day is a tango between brainstorming and hands-on making. I might be coming up with a concept for the next collection, doing image research and sketches, thinking up a catchy phrase for this and that, planning a performance to present the collection, building a set of window display, designing and hand-making leather products, pattern cutting, making a dramatic showpiece, rehearsing for a theatre show, then finally, at night I get to chill out with my guitar and write a song...

What is the wildest/craziest design practice you have done over the years?

Kay: I lose track because we always seem to be doing crazy things, but I think putting together the "Good Night Deer" show at the London Institute of Contemporary Art was probably the craziest thing we've done. We flew the entire collection over to London, and then rehearsed like mad with our team of 50+ people: a full production crew, make-up and hair artists, models, dressers, musicians...It was a very labor-intensive show! But it is so rewarding to put on a show like that, and we love the adrenaline rush that comes with the challenge...

Jing: Well yes, we've done major shows in London and performed letter-burning rituals on the streets of Hong Kong, but actually I think we're still being too safe. Wait till we open our first flagship store in Hong Kong this October! Finally we'll have our own space to create crazy displays, gigs and performances. It's going to be such an explosion of creativity. I can't wait!

Recy-couture
Styling
Collaboration with
Codesign and Heiwa
Paper Co.
Photography: Jimmy
Ming Shum

Please describe a moment/thing/person that has a strong influence on your work.

Jing: Kay, my sister. Without her I would never have started making clothes. I began as a theatre set designer, so my approach to fashion design is very much influenced by my sense of 3D space and construction.

Kay: My dad. He passed away 10 years ago, and I sometimes feel we didn't say goodbye properly, but I really believe he passed on his "dreamer" DNA to us, and that his spirit lives on in Daydream Nation

What has been repeatedly used in your artwork?

We often draw inspiration from stories, fairy-tales, books and films. For Kay, the starting point is more tactile: the material, texture, yarn...For Jing, it's more conceptual: the love of strong silhouettes and 3D shapes, and most importantly, translating story elements into visual and wearable garments.

What does your work teach you?

Jing: You don't have to"know", you just have to "do". That's how you learn.

Kay: Work has taught me that people are

everything. There is a Chinese song that goes "一枝竹仔会易折弯，几枝竹一扎断节难 " (One bamboo stick is easy to break, several is difficult)". We really believe that a dream you dream alone stays a dream; a dream you dream together is reality. We don't want this to just be about Jing and me, we want to create a "United Kingdom of dreamers and lovers".

Who is the No.1 leading-edge designer in your mind? Ask him/her a question.

Kay: Hussein Chalayan: "Where does your courage come from?"

Jing: Victor & Rolf: "What's the first thing you do when you start a collection?"

What makes you say "wooow!!" lately?

The movie "Inception".

What's the most important to you now?

Kay: Opening Daydream Nation the store!!

Jing: To stay awake while executing dreams.

SS10 Girl by the Sea
2010
Photography: Topaz Leung

AW09 Letter to Paul
2009
Photography: Franklin Lau

AW08 Good Night Deer
2008
Photography: Kevin Wong

SS08 Good Morning I'm Sleeping
2008

AW10 Boy on the Tree
2010
Photography by Tsi Kwan @ Picto

Recy-couture
Styling
Collaboration with
Codesign and Heiwa
Paper Co.
Photography:
Jimmy Ming Shum

FROM TIMBER:
TO PAPER:
I WONDER
WHAT
HAPPENS NEXT?

I reach towards the sky with my stems and leaves
breathing in the soft air and gentle sunlight.

100%
Post Consumer
Recycled

FSC Certified
Papers

Printed on 2307-300 Neenah Classic Crest 凝質紙 / 26" x 40" / 216gsm / Recycled Bright White

FROM TIMBER
TO PAPER:
I WONDER
WHAT
HAPPENS NEXT?

100%
Post Consumer
Recycled

FSC Certified
Papers

Slowly, I build my mass and become wood.
I wait for the moment to shed
my outer covering and become skins of paper.

desres is a design and consultancy studio and is active in a wide range of projects across a growing variety of media. desres projects feature concept, design, illustration, interactive design, typography, and art direction along with experience in film, installations, and moving images. desres works for corporate, cultural, and private clients as well as for advertising and event agencies. desres also engages in collaboration with other companies and professionals.

desres

What's your favorite part of your day?

Well, on the one hand I like the nights, because everything is so sensible and vulnerable at night. On the other hand I like the freshness of the early morning, when everything seems to be new and full of chances. Workingwise I prefer the morning, when there is no telephone ringing and I can put my headphones on and just work on my recent projects...

What is the wildest/craziest design practice you have done over the years?

To go on and on.

Please describe a moment/thing/person that has a strong influence on your work.

Besides many others my mum and dad are the persons who have most influenced my career. They taught me to be autonomous and have always encouraged me to do what I really love to do.

What has been repeatedly used in your artwork?

Typography.

What does your work teach you?

That every problem has hundreds of solutions.

Who is the No.1 leading-edge designer in your mind? Ask him/her a question?

Wow. There are so many good and even leading-edge (whatever that means) designers around the world. I would ask everyone and especially why he still does it...

What makes you say "wooow!!" lately?

There were two things during the last two weeks. One was the "Typo-Painting" the BERG did with the light of an iPad. The other was "The Journal of Popular Noise".

What's the most important to you now?

To be autonomous.

Westfluegel Magazine 01 –
Whim
Self-initiated Magazine
2009

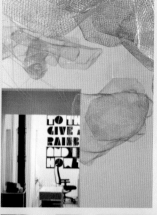

Cloud Cuckoo Land
Environmental graphics
2010
Collaboration with
Sounds of Silence

"To be autonomous."

Pooled Music –
Returned Series 03
Music packaging
2007

Pooled Music –
Returned Series 01
Music packaging
2006 – 2007

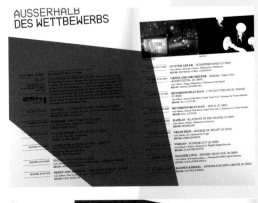

Filmtage Frankfurt
Visual identity/
Environmental graphics
2010

Deutsche & Japaner studio was initiated in 2008 and offers expertise in various disciplines, such as graphic design, product design, interior design, illustration and scenography as well as conceptual creation and strategic brand escort.

The studio focuses on communication, regardless of its physical condition, environmental, haptical or visual, but always in regard of sustainable experiences.

Ten Words and One Shot
CI/Book
2011

"...making 'better mistakes'."

Deutsche
&
Japaner

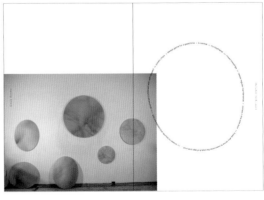

How did you join together as Deutsche & Japaner?

D&J was founded by Ina Yamaguchi and Moritz Firchow originally. Having known each other for quite a long time, they started doing projects together so founding the office was a logical conclusion. Joined by David Wolpert and Julian Zimmermann in 2010, we now feel very comfortable with our composition.

Moritz, if Julian were a smell, what would it be?

Probably a peanut butter jelly sandwich mixed with herbal notes of a drop deTerre d'Hermès.

David, if Ina were a shape, what would it be?

A Penrose triangle.

Ina, if Moritz were a sound, what would it be?

Biggie Smalls meets double click.

Julian, if David were a color, what would it be?

Red-blonde-army-green-camouflage.

How do you share the workload and work together since your specialties are different (communication design and industrial design)?

Depending on the project, we separate and team up for the best combination. If a

project is concentrated on interior solutions, it makes sense to build a team able to develop furniture and scenography. As for the graphic part we influence each other while we clearly all have certain emphases and side skills like a strong focus on typography, photography or coding etc.

What is the wildest/craziest design practice you have done over the years?

What happens at Deutsche & Japaner stays at Deutsche & Japaner. Everything else can be seen on our website.

Please describe a moment/thing/person that has a strong influence on your work.

That is not an easy question to answer, especially since we are several people. There are so many influences from fashion to architecture, music, furniture, arts and in history of course by all means. References are very important from our point of view, meaning wanting to create something unique needs profound knowledge.

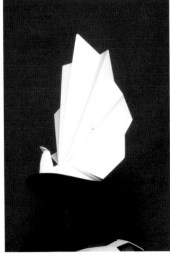

PAVOBLANC
Art direction/CI
2009

What does your work teach you?

Maybe one thing is to listen closely to one's needs, another is to be convincing about the importance of communication and building an aura of sensibility to all variables at all times. And quoting a friend of ours, making "better mistakes."

Who is the No.1 leading-edge designer in your mind? Ask him/her a question.

This is not fair! We know so many ambitious and ingenious people; it would be inadequate to only name some twenty here. Only naming 1 is a mission impossible.

What makes you say "wooow!!" lately?

The Qompendium publication;
Artworks by Swyndle and Hawks;
The "Back Room – Adults Only" installation and the new NZZ-Redesign by Mike Meiré;
Photography by Stephen Shore;
A statement by Matteo Thun.

What's the most important to you now?

Consolidating and building while enjoying work.

IGNORANT
CI
2011

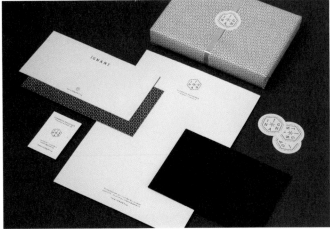

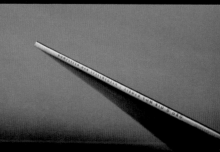

Vanitas Nullum
Art direction/Editorial/Poster
2011

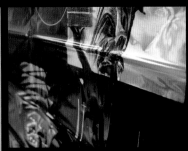

180 GRAD
Art direction
2010
Photography: D.W.
Schmalow

je ne regretted rien
(Self-initiated)
Product
2010

Driv Loo

Dreams Factory
VI/Typography
2009

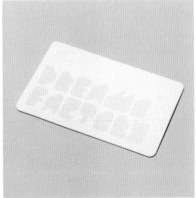

Boy and Girl
Lenticular poster
2007

"We tend to be wilder when we got nothing to lose. Don't think, just jump. That's the spirit!"

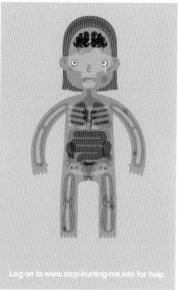

Not every cry for help is apparent.

Log on to www.stop-hurting-me.info for help.

What is the wildest/craziest design practice you have done over the years?

I remember I sprained my leg as I jumped off the second floor to shoot a chase scene for an assignment during my college years. We tend to be wilder when we got nothing to lose. Don't think, just jump. That's the spirit!

Do you have any role models for your design career?

The person you work with during the early years of your career is going to affect you so much in the future. I really appreciate and learn a lot from all the good people whom I've worked with so far. And they eventually became my role models too.

What has been repeatedly used in your artwork?

Simple, honest yet a little bit fun elements.

What does your work teach you?

As a designer I have to be more patient, be organized, and need to know how to present and express my thoughts. And most importantly, always stay interesting.

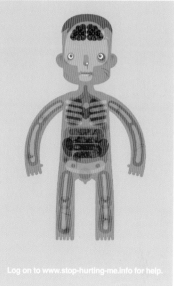

Not every cry for help is apparent.

Log on to www.stop-hurting-me.info for help.

Driv is a graphic designer. Born in Malaysia in 1983, he loves design, illustration, typography and always enjoys thinking stupid ideas. He is currently based in Singapore - still "staying stupid."

Smiley
Self-Initiated
2007

Dreams Factory
VI/Typography
2009

<u>Who is the No.1 leading-edge designer in your mind? Ask him/her a question.</u>

There are too many of them. The person who inspired me a lot recently is Kashiwa Sato. I admired his ability in handling different projects in different fields at the same time yet still making them all great. His book "Ultimate Method for Reaching the Essentials" teaches me a lot and now I'm still forcing myself to be more efficient at work.

<u>What makes you say "wooow!!" lately?</u>

Old Spice body wash commercials. Haha, I can't remember how many times I laugh at it. The 184 YouTube videos responded real time on the internet is an epic stunt; I think it's worth a Guinness world record.

<u>What's the most important to you now?</u>

Answer the last question for this Q&A.

Men's Uno
Fashion Illustration
2010

Window Gallery
Environmental graphics
2008

Chris Holzinger AW09 Lookbook
Editorial
2009

"We avoid repeating concepts or elements. For us it's important that each design has its own individual concept and visual appearance."

Eps51 is an internationally active design studio covering a wide range of projects including print, web, brand identity, illustration and photography. Before settling down in Berlin, Ben and Sascha lived and worked in London, Paris, Brussels and Cairo for a while. Eps51 have worked on numerous intercultural projects over the past years, mostly for clients from the cultural field.

How did you get the name Eps51?	When we founded Eps51 we were living in ErbPrinzenStr.51.
What is the wildest/craziest design practice you have done over the years?	We designed invitation cards for the re-opening of a tax consultant office which had renovated their office accommodations.
What has been repeatedly used in your artwork?	We avoid repeating concepts or elements. For us it's important that each design has its own individual concept and visual appearance.
What distinguishes your work from that of your contemporaries?	Does it?
A leading-edge designer in your mind? Ask him/her a question.	David Johnston: When are we gonna get the 150 quid you still owe us?
What is the best part of being a designer?	Having to deal with various kinds of subjects and people. Every single project is different which is why we constantly get involved with clients from diverse fields of activities.
What would you like to be if you were not a designer?	A Fat Cat, a Pro Skater or maybe Teenie Popstars?
What makes you say "wooow!!" recently?	360 Donald Russell.

Hang Holzinger
Outdoor AD
2009

Michael Sontag
CI
2010

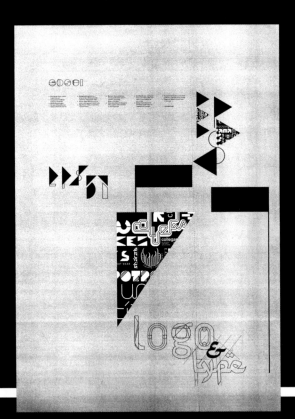

Eps51 Brownbook Poster
Poster for an exhibition in
Dubai
2008

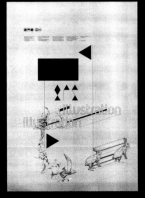

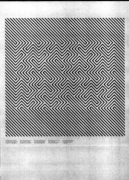

**Shirts – Willau™ and
Spokes**
Product
2008-2009

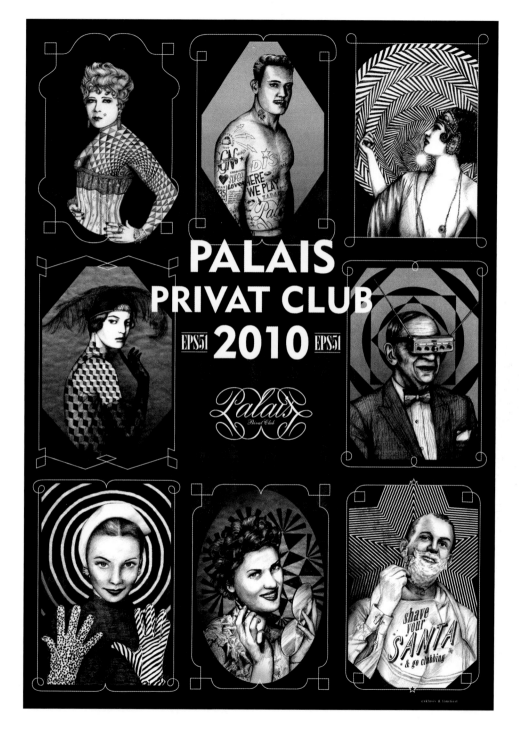

Esther Lee

What does your typical day look like?

Usually, after a relaxed breakfast I would go to my art studio to do work. After dinner, around 7:30 pm I go to swim. (I just love swimming!) At 9:30 pm, I put on some music and work or sometimes I go to movies with friends. As I am busy, I try to go to bed early because I focus on/ produce my work better when I work early in the morning.

What is the wildest/craziest design practice you have done over the years?

I don't know if I have the boldness to create such works. I work based on visual graphics and for the first time I created a mobile and table-formed structure this year. It wasn't easy making something three-dimensional from flat surface work; making a sturdy base to hold the object, hanging it horizontally, the choice of material, coloring, etc. – these weren't familiar to me so it took some effort. And I will be exhibiting this at Maison & Objet in Paris this September. I feel quite strange but I am pretty sure I will enjoy it and it will be a good experience for me.

Do you have any role models for your design career?

I do admire many great artists and I try to follow their passion of never ceasing to enjoy working on their art until they die. Maybe that would be the happiest life one can achieve.

What has been repeatedly used in your artwork?

I would describe my style as primary color oriented, limited color usage, repetitious, and pattern and character oriented.

What does your work teach you?

I avoid too pretty or too cute styles of work. But it is not easy to create sophisticated and humorous projects. It is usual that after the work is created, either you don't like it or you're already bored with it. Matter of length of work isn't important to me but it is necessary to take time to view your work with objectivity to mature your work.

I heard an author in South Korea saying her work makes her so embarrassed, every time she has new book out there, she would need a hundred pen names and this is so true to me.

Who is the No.1 leading-edge designer in your mind? Ask him/her a question.

I don't know if I can pin point one but rather I admire art of artists who portray their own characters into their work. Anyway I do not believe in No. 1 and can't fit to measure in art.

I love the flatness, color and formation of Henri Matisse, Marc Chagall's daydreaming pictures, and Alexander Calder's bold color of contrast on huge sculptures and mobiles. I love amazing giant stainless steel works of Jeff Koons and works of Roy Lichtenstein. I also love the fashion world of Marc Jacobs. There are so many people who work on great arts, whether they are designers, architects or artists.

What makes you say "wooow!!" lately?

Music that moves you! Great movies! A true heart! Especially, music that takes me into an extreme, pleasant state of emotion.

Esther Lee takes great pleasure out of rhythmic and repetitive forms.

She is also fond of plastic products with vivid colors like the color of bananas.

She was born in Seoul and studied advertising design at Hong-Ik University.

She has been creating works based on the relationship between images and patterns as an illustrator and graphic designer.

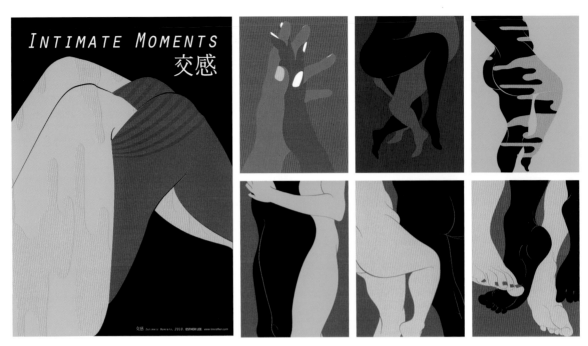

Intimate Moments
Illustration
2010

What's the most important to you now?

Basically, I try to make my life abundant in quality and value. And I like to enjoy it as I work...I want to establish my life with purpose and be more broad-minded. This is my main focus in my life now. I hope to have a prosperous exhibition at the Maison & Objet in September, putting my best.

***Planet, Diamonds,
Super Glue Etc.***
Exhibition
2008

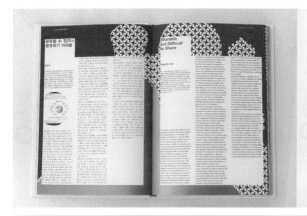

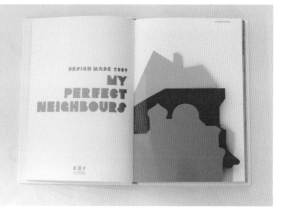

My Perfect Neighbors
Poster/Illustration
2009

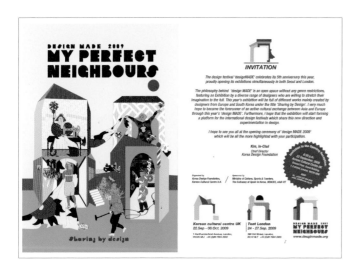
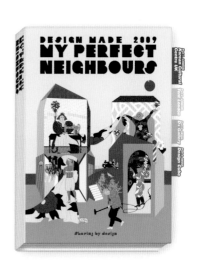

**A Yellow Rabbit in the
Kaleidoscope Eyes**
Art direction/Exhibition
2009

"I do admire many great artists and I try to follow their passion of never ceasing to enjoy working on their art until they die. Maybe that would be the happiest life one can achieve."

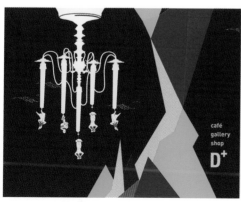

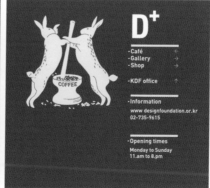

Franca Moor

Franca Moor is a designer living in Lucerne, Switzerland. In September 2009, she graduated from the Graphic Design major at Lucerne.

Genius has mastered chaos, so she's thinking order is only something for dummies. She gets up at 6 am. She swims daily in restless water and she's still alive thanks to daydreams. She loves to dive in her screen-deep-sea between punches and serifs. For desserts she prefers raspberry jelly and fine typography. She's glad about the triumph of the printed word and about the white and black keys of her piano. She loves screen-printing, her risographs in the basement, playing with typography and enjoying her life.

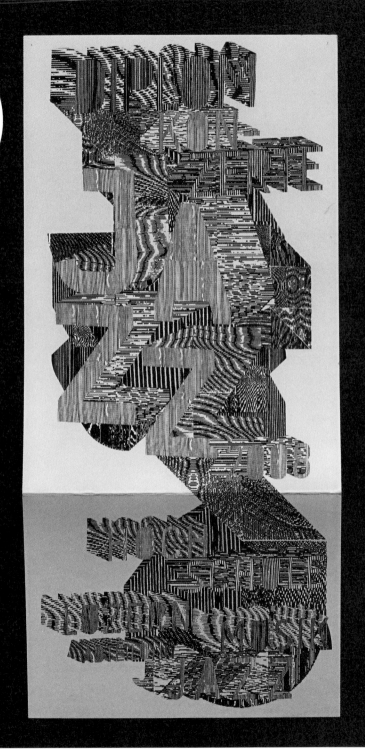

Bachelor Concerts Music Academy Luzern
Poster
2009
Collaboration with Samuel Egloff

What's your favorite part of your day?

Midnight hour – witching hour.

What is the wildest/craziest design practice you have done over the years?

I think this was the Jazz poster for the Bachelor concerts of the music academy in Lucerne. I worked with Samuel Egloff on this project. We started analogue with experiments on an old letterpress printing machine. With the backside of the wooden letters we generated new letters, after further experiments on the copier we scanned the results and worked on our computers. With screenshots we finally came to our structure.

Please describe a moment/thing/person that has a strong influence on your work.

Every new day is full of new inspiration that influence my work. This diversity of new inputs is what I really appreciate at my profession.

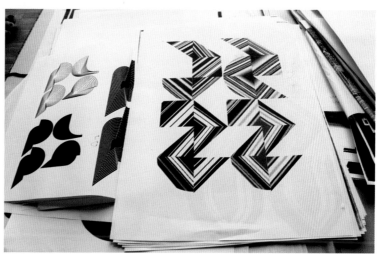

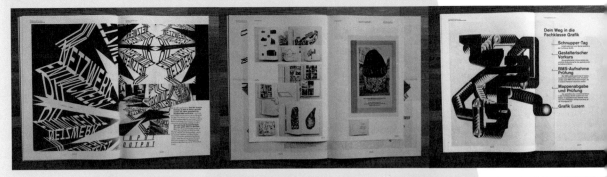

What has been repeatedly used in your artwork?

Tools are depending on the project. These may be scanner, paper and scissor, copier, camera, aeroso, laptop...In the beginning it's like doing handicrafts. After I scan or photograph my objects I start working on the computer. It's the way I often came to unexpected solutions and that's the way I love to work.

What does your work teach you?

Stay strong, stay serious, stay genius, stay funny: stay controlled and lose control.

Who is the No.1 leading-edge designer in your mind? Ask him/her a question.

Simon Trüb. Do you believe in ghosts?

What makes you say "wooow!!" lately?

To see somebody dancing on a high wire.

What's the most important to you now?

To go on.

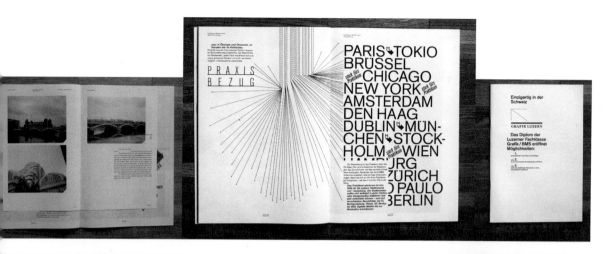

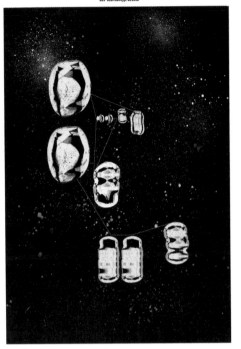

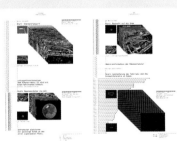

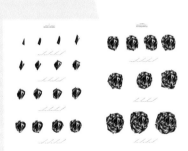

UND DEINE FREUNDE WERDEN
SEHR ERSTAUNT SEIN WENN SIE
SEHEN, *DASS DU DEN HIMMEL*
ANBLICKST UND LACHST. DANN
WIRST DU IHNEN SAGEN:
„*JA, DIE STERNE DIE BRINGEN*
MICH IMMER ZUM LACHEN!"
UND SIE WERDEN DICH FÜR
VERRÜCKT HALTEN.

WIE DEIN STERN AUSZUSEHEN
HAT BESTIMMST ALLEINE DU:
001-004: SILEXA[1], SENSILIX[2],
ANYLIX[3] ODER SYNTEX[4].

1 2 3 4

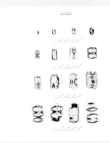

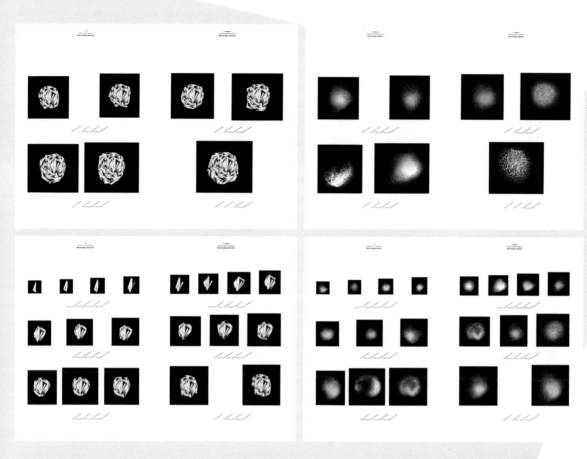

**Be a Star Forever
(self-initiated)**
Magazine
2009

„WIE KANN MAN STERNE BESITZEN?"
„WEM GEHÖREN SIE?" ERWIDERTE ICH.
„ICH WEISS NICHT. NIEMANDEM."
„DANN GEHÖREN SIE MIR, ICH HABE
ALS ERSTER DARAN GEDACHT."
„DAS GENÜGT?"
„GEWISS. WENN DU EINEN DIAMANTEN
FINDEST, DER NIEMANDEM GEHÖRT,
SO IST ER DEIN. WENN DU EINE IN-
SEL FINDEST DIE NIEMANDEM GEHÖRT
SO IST SIE DEIN. WENN DU ALS
ERSTER EINEN EINFALL HAST UND DU
LÄSST IHN PATENTIEREN, SO IST ER
DEIN. UND ICH, ICH BESITZE DIE
STERNE, DA NIEMAND VOR MIR DARAN
GEDACHT HAT, SIE ZU BESITZEN."

Antoine de Saint-Exupéry

"100 beste Plakate, Deutschland, Österreich, Schweiz" Exhibition, Luzern
Poster/Flyer
2010

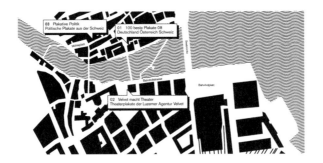

WELTFORMAT 09
Plakatfestival Luzern

Wie gross die Wirkung von Plakaten nach wie vor ist, zeigen die jüngsten Diskussionen. Der Verein «Posters Lucerne» hat sich zum Ziel gesetzt, dieses Medium zu fördern und dessen Vielfalt einem breiten Publikum näher zu bringen. Gerade die Schweiz mit ihrer langen Tradition im Plakatschaffen und einem einzigartigen Plakatformat, Weltformat genannt, braucht ein Plakatfestival mit internationaler Ausstrahlung. Das Festival

„Weltformat 09" gliedert sich in drei Teile:

Zum siebten Mal zeigen wir die «100 besten Plakate – Deutschland, Österreich, Schweiz» in Luzern. Der zweite Ausstellungsteil ist die Retrospektive «velvet macht theater» und der dritte setzt sich mit dem politischen Pfakat der Schweiz «Plakative Politik» auseinander.

Wir danken folgenden Partnern für Ihre Unterstützung:

- Stadt Luzern
- FUKA-Fonds Stadt Luzern
- APG Affichage Luzern
- Hochschule Luzern – Design & Kunst
- Von Ah Druck Stans
- Auviso Luzern
- Luzerner Theater
- Castelli Reklame AG
- Basler Plakatsammlung
- Niklaus Troxler
- AWP AG Kriens

Verein Posters Lucerne
Wenn Sie sich für das Medium Plakat engagieren möchten, sollten Sie Mitglied bei Posters Lucerne werden. Der Verein ist im Aufbruch, benötigt finanzielle Unterstützung und bietet den Mitgliedern die Möglichkeit, die Zukunft des Plakats in der Schweiz aktiv mit zu gestalten.

Mitgliedsbeiträge pro Jahr
Plakatfreunde: 100.- CHF
Ateliers/Firmen/Vereine: 250,-
Studierende: ein Tag Freiwilligenarbeit

---

1. 100 Besten Plakate 08
Deutschland, Österreich, Schweiz
Kornschütte Kornmarkt 3

Posters Lucerne zeigt zum siebten Mal exklusiv in der Schweiz die Siegerplakate des Wettbewerbs „100 Beste Plakate–Deutschland Österreich Schweiz". Die Jury (Vorsitz: FLAG Aubry/Broquard, Grafik-Designer, CH Zürich, mit Cordula Ales-sandri, Grafik-Designerin, A Wien / Georg Barber, Grafik-Designer/Illustrator, D Berlin / Dr. Anita Kühnel, Kunsthistorikerin, D Berlin / Christian Lagé, Grafik-Designer, D Berlin) wählte aus 1521 eingereichten Plakaten aus. Wie in den letzten Jahren ist der Anteil der Schweizer Sieger/innen überproportional hoch.

2. Velvet macht Theater
Theaterplakate der Luzerner Agentur Velvet
Luzerner Theater Theaterstr.2

Seit 1999 arbeitet Velvet als Kommunikationsagentur für Theater. Zuerst waren es Plakatkampagnenfür das Luzerner Theater, die vom Eidgenössischen Departement des Innern als "beste Plakatkampagne der Schweiz" ausgezeichnet wurden. Später wird Velvet

Agentur der Münchner Kammerspiele, des Theaters Freiburg und des Schauspiels Köln. Ihre Plakate sorgen für viel Wirbel und Publizität, und werden mit internationalen Preisen überhäuft. In der Multimediapräsentation werden die Theaterarbeiten von Velvet im Kontext der öffentlichen Wahrnehmung gezeigt.

www.velvet.ch

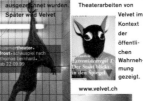

3. Plakative Politik
Politische Plakate aus der Schweiz
HSLU Design & Kunst
Rössligasse 12

Im politischen Plakat spiegelt sich der gesellschaftliche Wandel in vieler Hinsicht. Wie provokativ politische Plakate sein können, bewies das SVP-Plakat zur Minarettinitiative, das im Abstimmungs- und Wahlkampf eingesetzt wurde, gibt es heute auch Plakate, die für humanitäre und karitative Werke werben

oder sich der Umweltproblematik widmen. in Konfrontation zu anderen Plakaten mit dem gleichen Thema gezeigt

Rapunzel Goes Independent
Poster
2010

Work Show at
Fachklasse Grafik Luzern
Poster
2010

Werkschau
2010

Samstag 3. bis   Fachklasse Grafik
Mittwoch 7. Juli   Rösslgasse 12
Vernissage: **Freitag,** 6000 Luzern 5
2. Juli, 18 Uhr

Die Fachklasse zeigt, was sie kann: Vom Illustrations-
projekt des 1. bis zur Diplomarbeit des 3. Studienjahrs.
Mit Bar- und Grillbetrieb im Innenhof. Alle sind eingeladen.

Öffnungszeiten:
Samstag, Sonntag 10 – 18 Uhr
Montag, Dienstag 10 – 20 Uhr
Mittwoch 10 – 22 Uhr

Sonder-
ausstellungen

Zwischen Hammer   **Lichtblicke:**
und Amboss: Theres Bütler, im Foyer,
Tino Steinemann, in   Rösslgasse 12
der Metallwerkstatt,
Rösslgasse 12

Theres Bütler und Tino Steinemann, zwei ventilierte
und geschätzte Dozierende der Fachklasse Grafik hatten
in vergangenen Studienjahr ihren letzten Unterrichtstag.
Beide fielen sich weit über Luzern hinaus einen Namen
gemacht, Theres als Fotografie, Tino als Grafiker. Zwei
Sonderausstellungen widmen sich ihrem vielfältigen und
ausgezeichneten Arbeiten.

Das volle
Programm

Samstag 3. bis   Erholungsraum
Mittwoch 7. Juli   Rösslgasse 12
                         6000 Luzern 5

Sterbtier, Segel setzen, auf zu neuen Ufern: Was
macht die Einzigartigkeit der Ausbildung an der Fachklasse
Grafik aus? Was lernen die Studierenden während der
Ausbildung, welche Projekte machen sie, wie entwickeln sie
sich vier jungen Talenten zu ausgezeichneten Grafikerinnen
und Grafikern? Im Erholungsraum stellt eine Diplomandin
die Projekte ihrer gestalterischen Ausbildung aus

Gestaltung: Franca Mina

Infotag an der
Werkschau

Dienstag 6. Juli   Erholungsraum
13 – 20 Uhr   Rösslgasse 12
                         6000 Luzern 5

Die Fachklasse Grafik stellt sich vor. Mit Informatio-
nen zu Ausbildung, Aufnahmeverfahren, Talentabklärung
und Laufbahnschritten. Der Infotag richtet sich an junge
Talente, interessierte Lehrer und Eltern. Mit individuellen
Informationsgesprächen.

Diplomfeier

Mittwoch 7. Juli   Gesellschaftshaus der
18.30 – 20 Uhr   Herren zu Schützen,
                         Löwengraben 24
                         6004 Luzern

Summa cum laude für junge Grafikerinnen und Grafiker! Zur Diplomfeier sind die Diplomandinnen und Diplo-
manden, ihre Angehörigen und die Dozierenden eingeladen. Im Anschluss findet im Innenhof der Rösslgasse ein
Apéro statt.

Weiter werden Förderpreise vergeben:
1. Zeugnisdesign-Preis 2010
2. Förderpreis SGD

Absolventinnen und Absolventen:

Amirthalingam   Sarton Marco /
Gowdhaman /   Scheidegger Pablo /
Büchler Simon /   Scherer Fabienne /
Egger Janine /   Schmitz Dominique /
Ehrler Solange /   Schmucki Dali /
Gillis Henry /   Stucki Carina /
Huber Elsa /   Unternährer Patrick /
Hürbin Alexandra /   Wicki Salomon /
Jung Julian /   Widmer Ivo /
Linder Lukas /   Wildhaber Carlo /
Lischer Diana /   Zehnder Angelina /
Nasupovic Nihad /   Zopfi Lena /
Renggli Simon /

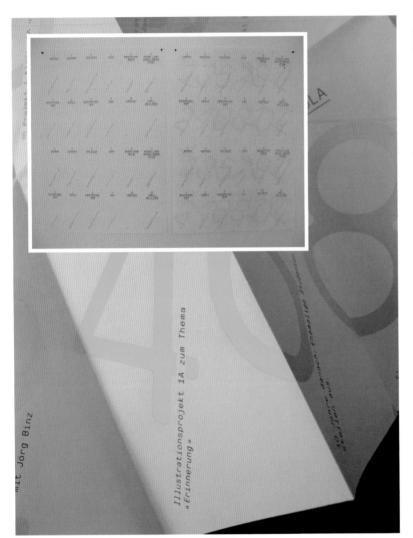

"Stay strong, stay serious, stay genius, stay funny: stay controlled and lose control."

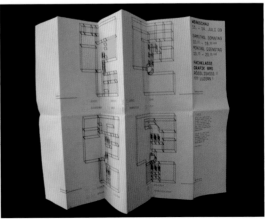

Frédérique
Daubal

What's your favorite part of your day?
Morning.

What is the wildest/craziest design practice you have done over the years?
Looking into trash and made the best out of it to be accepted by the client.

Please describe a moment/thing/person that has a strong influence on your work.
...

What has been repeatedly used in your artwork?
Fabrics, popular thoughts, ideas, old clothes.

What does your work teach you?
So many things... how to deal with so many different persons, be there, active, daring doing things...

Who is the No.1 leading-edge designer in your mind? Ask him/her a question.
I don't care that much about leading designers, lots of unknown people have fantastic small or big ideas and goals which has never been revealed for so many reasons. But when you link good ideas with brave people, it can be magic.

What makes you say "wooow!!" lately?
My kids or kids in general.

What's the most important to you now?
Feeling good - then I can face anything.

Respect, fighting for integration and good immigration, giving the same chance to kids, reading Claude lévi-strauss and trying to laugh a lot to be able to resist better.

After being a foreigner in different countries, mainly Montreal and The Nederlands, Frédérique Daubal is now biking in Paris. Coming from a graphic design background, she works as a freelance creative for small and large clients worldwide. She also experiments with textile as a 3 dimensional medium. She creates products under her name without following any trends. She has incorporated many secondhand pieces into her projects since she began designing in 2001. She focuses on personal artwork and collaborations with people and magazines mostly for experimental ideas, installations, and exhibitions.

129

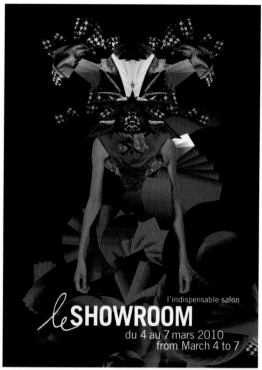

le Showroom
Poster/Installation
2009/2010

Hide & Seek
Art project
2010

Snake Expander
Illustration
2009/2010

Green Rainbow Kids
Installation
2008

Vicarini
VI/Edition
2007/2010

éclaircie en fin de journée

"... *when you link good ideas with brave people,
it can be magic.*"

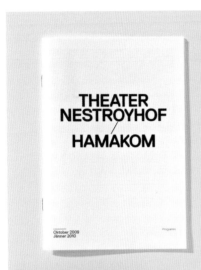

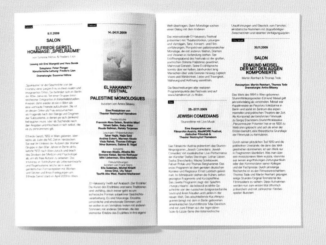

Grafisches Büro is a collective of three designers Günter Eder, Roman Breier and Marcel Neundörfer. Founded in 2003, they specialize in brand design and publications with a focus on typography, research and materials/ production.

Theater Nestroyhof Hamakom
Brand identity
2009-2011
Photography: Felix Friedmann, Marc
Glassner, Marcel van der Vlugt &
Yvonne Lacet

How did you meet each other and set up the studio?

Step 1: Roman met Günter.
Step 2: Working on projects together.
Step 3: Joining clients.
Step 4: Teaming up with Marcel.
Step 5: Working together.

What is the wildest/ craziest design practice you have done over the years?

The Wonderland book – printed with 22 colors.

Günter, if Marcel were a shape, what would it be?

A sine wave.

Roman, if Günter were a sound, what would it be?

Peep.

Marcel, if Roman were a typeface, what would it be?

Helveticade.

What has been repeatedly used in your artwork?

Mr. & Mrs. Helvetica.

The Cooked Kitchen
Book concept/Design
2008
Backlight Photography:
Paul Prada

What does your work teach you?

Design is attitude.
(Helmut Schmid)

Who is the No.1 leading-edge designer in your mind? Ask him/her a question.

Julia Born. - Everything´s ok?

What makes you say "wooow!!" lately?

Your invitation!

What's the most important to you now?

Quiet manner.

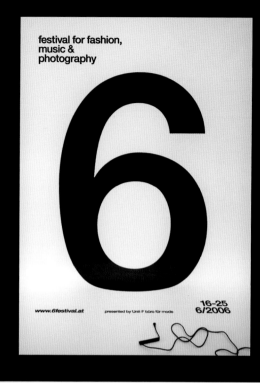

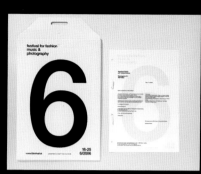

6, 7 – Festival for Fashion and Photography
Naming/Logo/Corporate design
2006-2007
Photography: Bettina Komenda
& Peter Garmusch

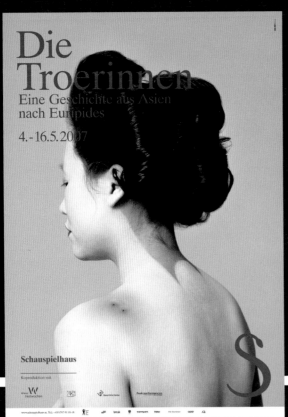

Die Troerinnen

Eine Geschichte aus Asien
nach Euripides

4.-16.5.2007

Schauspielhaus

Koproduktion mit

Schauspielhaus

21.3.-9.4.2006

Der Familientisch

9 Monate später

**Schauspielhaus
(Theatre Vienne)**
Poster
2004-2007
Photography: Jork Weismann
Post Production: Viennapaint

"Design is attitude. (Helmut Schmid)"

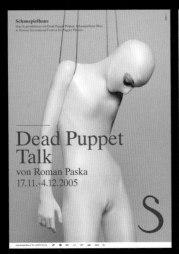

Schauspielhaus
Eine Koproduktion von Dead Puppet Project, Schauspielhaus Wien
& Hessen International Festival for Puppet Theatre

Dead Puppet Talk

von Roman Paska

17.11.-4.12.2005

Das verräterische Herz

//nach Edgar Allan Poe
15.04.-16.05.2004

Schauspielhaus

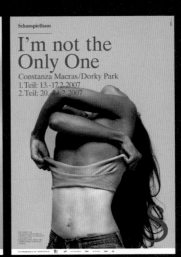

Schauspielhaus

I'm not the Only One

Constanza Macras/Dorky Park
1. Teil: 13.-17.2.2007
2. Teil: 20.-24.2.2007

Tadao Ando
Concept proposal
2008

Hamish Smyth is a 24 year old Australian based in New York City. He is currently working at Pentagram Design for Michael Bierut.

"Doing things you enjoy everyday."

Hamish, what does your typical day look like?

Right now I'm working full time at Pentagram in New York for Michael Bierut. My day can vary from working on tiny logos through to giant way-finding systems. It's an exciting environment to be in and I'm grateful to be surrounded by so many talented individuals.

What is the wildest/craziest design practice you have done over the years?

In university I decided it would be a good idea to graph all of the Australian Census data. It ended up taking weeks of solid work. Certainly not wild but definitely crazy.

What has been repeatedly used in your artwork?

I like to think all my work has a strong concept behind it – but in reality sometimes designers will make a decision based purely on aesthetics – I guess I'm not immune to that. I tend to have a pretty broad style however and do not tend to repeat myself too much – I hope!

What distinguishes your work from that of your contemporaries?

I didn't think my work is at all distinguished from my contemporaries. There are many amazing designers in the world. I'm constantly shocked by some people's talent and just a little bit jealous too.

A leading-edge designer in your mind? Ask him/her a question.

Well seeing as I'm at Pentagram I really want to ask Paula Scher what she thinks of the NY Art Directors Club rebranding. But

I'm too scared to ask…

<u>What is the best part of being a designer?</u>
Doing things you enjoy everyday.

<u>What makes you say "wooow!!" lately?</u>
Being in New York City! I'm pretty excited to be here – it's still quite surreal. I've also just back packed through Europe for four months and saw some spectacular things.

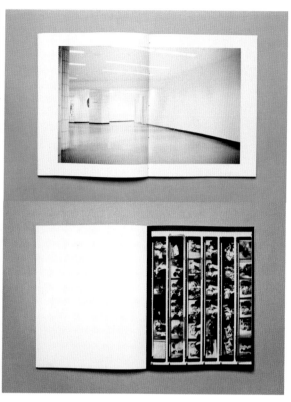

The three designers graduated from the Lucerne University of applied Sciences and Arts in 2008 and have worked since 2009 as HEKUZUKU. HEKUZUKU is a graphic design studio located in Zürich and composed of Marlon Ilg, Jill Mattes and Simon Trüb. HEKUZUKU conceives and creates products in the field of visual communication.

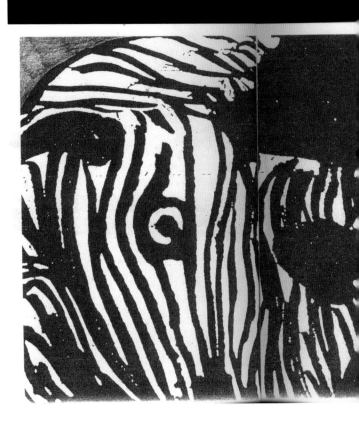

Wälde
Book/Illustration/Production
2009

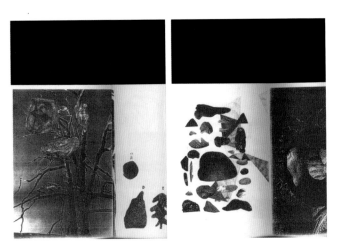

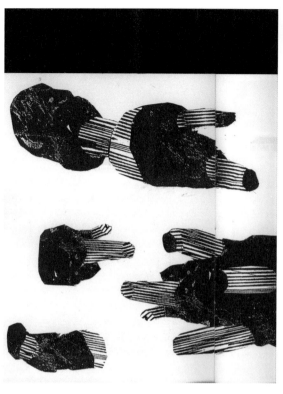

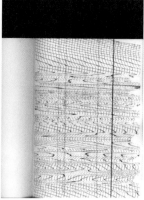

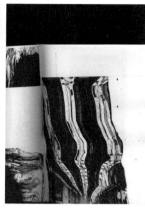

Species Profi
Book/Illustration/Production
2008

How did you get the name "Hekuzuku"?
Herkunft (origin) Zukunft (future) .

What is the wildest/craziest design practice you have done over the years?
24 × 7.

Please describe a moment/thing/person that has a strong influence on your work.
We feel connected to nature.

What has been repeatedly used in your artwork?
Handmade to copier. Copier to scanner. Scanner to computer. Computer to printer. Printer to trash. Try again.

What does your work teach you?
Get rich or die trying.

Who is the No.1 leading-edge designer in your mind? Ask him/her a question.
Jonas Vögeli, Körner Union, Yokoland. How many tries are ending in the trash until it fits?

What makes you say "wooow!!" lately?
Rene B. aka Dj Bobo in Action.

What's the most important to you now?
Our work & getting famous.

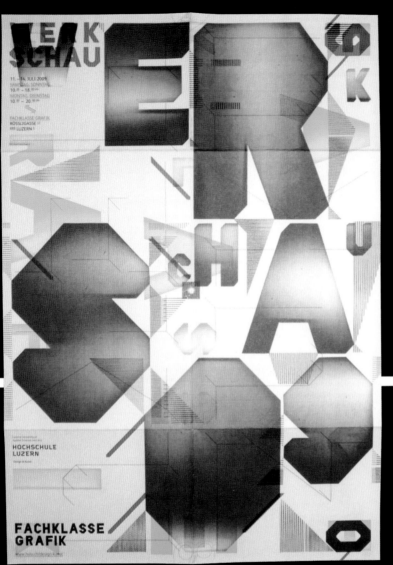

Werkschau
Poster/Flyer
2009

Habitat
(Self-initiatetd)
Book/Poster
2010
Collaboration with
Andreas Iten

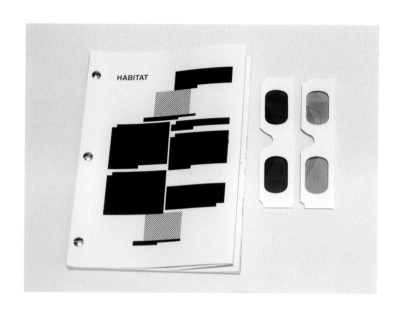

*"Handmade to copier. Copier to scanner. Scanner to computer.
Computer to printer. Printer to trash. Try again."*

HelloMe

HelloMe is a Berlin based graphic design practice set up by Till Wiedeck.

The studio focuses on the concept & creation of distinctive dynamic visual systems, based on research, strategy and creative thought. The practice is driven by curiosity and the belief in an original and innovative communication.

The studio specializes in graphic design and art direction with a passion for typography and simplicity, beautiful detail and a keen sense for aesthetics, believing that strong ideas form the basis for an exceptional design vocabulary.

Besides working for a variety of commercial and cultural clients, HelloMe is a playground for visual experiments, self-initiated projects and collaborations with like-minded people.

What does your typical day look like?

These days I am taking it a bit slow in the mornings as I realized that is the best time for me to get inspiration. What I really need on a good morning is to lie in bed for at least 30 min after waking up to just stare at the blank white ceiling. That is basically the time when I have most of my ideas. After breakfast and some sports I am finally ready to start working. Most of the time this means pushing graphic elements from A to B, doing layouts, developing typefaces, going to photo shoots, talking to clients, et cetera. I really like to involve the people I work with/for in the concept and design process. I think this is how both parties can build a strong relation to the project and its final outcome. Depending on the size and urgency of the project I leave the studio between 7 and 12pm to meet some friends, have a drink or take a ride around town on my bike.

What is the wildest/craziest design practice you have done over the years?

The most intense project I have been working on lately is "Hier & Dasein" which would translate into "Here & being there". It is the collaborative degree project of Henning Walther and myself. In "Hier & Dasein" we dealt with the theme Orientation and all its side effect and phenomena. Within four very intense months we worked our way through the theme. After a two months research phase we wrote and designed a book and created a series of art installations to abstractly visualize the different aspects of orientation. For these months we spend at least 8 to sometimes 24 hours a day working together. You could call it a social design experiment. But we made it and still are really good friends though.

Making Public
Visual identity/Posters/Catalogue
2010
Collaboration with Petri Henriksson &
BlankBlank.

Please describe a moment/thing/person that has a strong influence on your work.

I think the biggest influence on my work comes from the people surrounding me and which I feel a strong connection to. I think the personal influences automatically translate into the work one develops. So it comes naturally that good friends and partners always have a huge impact on my work. I guess especially my girlfriend who is a textile designer influences me. Sometimes more than I know.

What has been repeatedly used in your artwork?

I am a pretty big admirer of the early constructivism and suprematism. I use a lot of geometric stuff in my work. I also love working with mostly reduced color schemes. The most important part for me is probably typography but this is no wonder to me as I fell in love with type when I was about 10 years old and started writing graffiti. Nowadays I don't really feel a direct graffiti-influence in my work anymore. However it still is how I learned the basics of typography and about the power it has.

What does your work teach you?

Actually there are quite a few things I learned through work in the last years. I worked at several well known studios and with some really talented and lovely people. Through this I saw many different methods of operating. This really teaches me a lot about how I want to live and work in general. I realized a certain freedom is very important to me and decided to put my energy into my own studio which turned out to be a good decision so far. On another level I think working with clients and collaborators teaches you to take responsibility. Not only for yourself and your own work but most importantly for the clients and their needs. You have the responsibility to develop the best possible solutions for their problems. This often leads away from the drawing board and brings you to places which you did not think of before. It pushes your own boundaries, which is great.

Who is the No.1 leading-edge designer in your mind? Ask him/her a question.

I am not really good with role models. For example I love the product design work by Dieter Rams, who in my opinion still is one of the best designers in the world. He created a unique product system and design vocabulary which even after 40 years looks

like it was designed in 2010 because it uses simplicity and function as the number one rule. This I think is a true leading-edge designer but still only one of many.

What makes you say "wooow!!" lately?

Probably the biggest "wooow!!" was the Exhibition "Innen Stadt Aussen" by Olafur Eliasson at Martin-Gropius-Bau in Berlin this summer. I love how he connects art, science, design and architecture to become something in between. A real hybrid. Some might say it is just pop but I think his work has an impact on how people perceive their environment which in this intensity is rather rare.

What's the most important to you now?

Now I am focusing on running my own studio HelloMe. I have to take care of a lot of things on my own these days so I probably will have some people joining HelloMe in the future. Which is great, I love working in a team with talented and awesome people. On another level I get bored pretty fast so I always try to push myself and my work to another level. It keeps me moving which is also really important to me. Let's hope this will never stop.

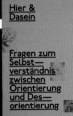

"*You have the responsibility to develop the best possible solutions for their (clients') problems. This often leads away from the drawing board and brings you to places which you did not think of before. It pushes your own boundaries, which is great.*"

Hudson-Powell

KylieX2008
Tour visuals
2008

Formed in 2005 by brothers Jody and Luke, Hudson-Powell is a design studio working in print, interactive and motion graphics. Both Luke and Jody studied Graphic Design at Central Saint Martins with Jody going on to do the Virtual Environments MSC at Bartlett School of Architecture. The studio's design principles focus on the dual development of concept and medium with clients in the arts, education and business. The studio also works on self-initiated projects which have been shown at various exhibitions including "Brno Echo" at the Moravian Gallery (CZ), "Forms of Inquiry" (UK, FR, CH), and in the solo show "Responsive Type" at SoSo gallery (JP).

Grazing Jellies
Augmented reality installation
2010

Time Base Arts
Visual identity/Branding
2010

What's your favourite part of your day?

When things get quiet towards the end of the day and you can actually design, a lot of the day can be sucked up with studio tasks. I also like the bits of the day when I'm riding my bike, hanging out with my girlfriend, having an idea, or eatin'...?

What is the wildest/craziest design practice you have done over the years?

We questioned the sanity of stuffing thousands of tiny foam balls into small handmade pouches to attach to a homemade virtual reality headset. Also standing in a forest while it rained down whistling to cosmic slugs as they ate watermelon, that felt pretty odd.

Please describe a moment/thing/person that has a strong influence on your work.

We both like to read up on science, technology and archaeology, so our influence often comes from the past and an imagined future. Recently we've been inspired by socially motivated projects too,

design sometimes forgets its responsibility to society, so it's good to be reminded that design is capable of making people's lives better.

What has been repeatedly used in your artwork?

We have trust in process, reference history and nature, and use a lot of geometries..? A friend told me that he thought the theme that ran through our work was simply that it was experimental.

What does your work teach you?

That there is rarely only one solution to anything.

Who is the No.1 leading-edge designer in your mind? Ask him/her a question.

The guy who is currently developing the landing system for the EJSM unmanned space mission to Jupiter's ice moons Europa. Is it still as exciting a job as you imagined it would be when you were 8?

ASOS HIT
Visual identity/
Branding
2009

<u>What makes you say "wooow!!" lately?</u>

Someone opening their car door on me and nearly knocking me off my bicycle the other day.

<u>What's the most important to you now?</u>

Getting things out of our heads and into the world + Growing tomatoes and chillies.

UNIQLO
T-shirt design
2008

"Recently we've been inspired by socially motivated projects too, design sometimes forgets its responsibility to society, so it's good to be reminded that design is capable of making people's lives better."

The Art of Conversation
Exhibit
2010

Inventory
Studio

Puma Rewind Forward
Pop-out shop
2010
A project conceived collaboratively between
Inventory Studio, Eat Sleep Work/Play and
The Klassnik Corporation. Constructed by
Wilder Creative.

Inventory Studio

What's your favorite part of your day?

The morning, the beginning of a new day.
Cycling to the studio with cold air/sunshine
on my face.

What is the wildest/craziest design practice
you have done over the years?

If a "crazy" idea works then it was actually
just an unexpected solution.

We were recently asked by Puma to design
interiors for a Pop-Up Shop that would visit
a number of UK cities and festivals, we

went back to them with an architect and
a concept to build a bespoke fitted truck
that could be both the destination and the
transportation for the content. Don't think
outside the box. There is no box.

Please describe a moment/thing/person
that has a strong influence on your work.

I guess going "to work" with my father
when I was younger has influenced me. He
is a trained carpenter and amateur inventor
with a natural D.I.Y approach to problem
solving; he built a speedboat when I was

very young. It didn't last long but the trial and error approach and the lack of the fear of failure has stayed with me.

What has been repeatedly used in your artwork?

A conceptual approach and a desire to make good things great.

What does your work teach you?

Whenever possible we will try to use a new process/material/aesthetic that is suited to the particulars of the brief. Involving experimentation with (image making) processes in our practice means we are constantly learning and growing as designers and problem solvers.

Who is the No.1 leading-edge designer in your mind? Ask him/her a question.

For a diverse body of work that defies definition: Heatherwick Studio (Thomas Heatherwick).

I'd ask him what he thought about opening a school.

What makes you say "wooow!!" lately?

Simplicity.

What's the most important to you now?

Being lucky enough to do what I want with my life makes me even keener to help others along their way.

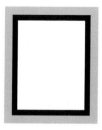

Inventory Studio is a London based design consultancy founded by Robert Boon and David Lane in December 2008. Inventory Studio art directs and designs projects for commercial and cultural clients, consults brands on creative strategy, conceives and curates exhibitions and events, runs workshops, gives talks and designs and produces editions and products.

The Art of Conversation: London—Berlin
Exhibition design
2010
Collaboration with BANK (Berlin).

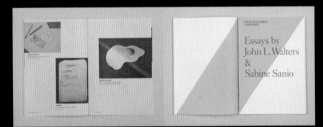

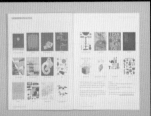

"Whenever possible we will try to use a new process/ material/aesthetic that is suited to the particulars of the brief. Involving experimentation with (image making) processes in our practice means we are constantly learning and growing as designers and problem solvers."

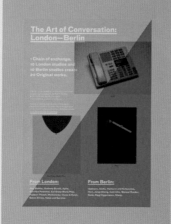

Jean Jullien is a French graphic designer living and working in London. He comes from Nantes and got a graphic design degree in Quimper before coming to London. He graduated from Central Saint Martins in 2008 and from the Royal College of Art in 2010.

He works closely with the musician Niwouinwouin. His practice ranges from illustration to photography, video, costumes, installations, books, posters and clothing to create a coherent yet eclectic body of work.

Portrait Photography: Akihito Igarashi

News of the Times
Poster/Book
2010

Jean Jullien

What does your typical day look like?

Well it's going to sound lame but my days are never the same. Especially since I finished college. I travel for shows and exhibitions, I work with different people, and every project is different from the other. It's amazing to be able to never get bored with your work. There are certain elements of routine that are very welcomed though, as they give a hint of structure: waking up not so early, checking emails and spending a lot of time replying to them, then a lot of traveling (going from one place to the other, from a photo studio to a gallery space to an agency, etc...) and working in the same time, taking most of my day. There's a lot of playing games also (pool, darts, cards, etc...) because that's just good sense to spend time having fun. Then usually going out at night and doing a lot of my illustration/ desk work late at night. I work well at night.

What is the wildest/craziest design practice you have done over the years?

I find projects that involve people, in general, to be the hardest. Very interesting though. It's an experience. The short film "The Normality Issue" and the staged narrative "Yann" were amongst the most stupid/ difficult/ hard projects I've done. Working with so many people can be very difficult when you lack experience like me.

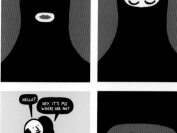

The exhibition "The Village" was a pretty crazy project too: creating an upside down village with a house hung onto the ceiling. We (the amazing Tom Lovell & me) did it in a week and put a stupid amount of effort into it. No way could I have done this on my own.

But, in term of craziness, the project Adventures in Front of the TV set, which Niwouinwouin and I have created is about the craziest work I've had to do. Animation requires such patience, and the technical aspects (4 giant screens, live music and video, interactivity, etc...) are pretty heavy to take on. Add the live experience, dealing with the audience etc, and you realize how far from the drawing table you are...

Please describe a moment/thing/person that has a strong influence on your work.

People who managed to convey great ideas in minimal ways. On the top of my mind: Raymond Savignac, Tomi Ungerer, Sempé. Wittiness, that's one thing to look up to.

Working with my brother Niwouinwouin is also very influential. We share the same universe/ culture so we know exactly where each other's idea comes from, we just express it differently in our own medium. It gives a great relevance to the critic we can both make about the other's work. It's like a subconscious critic. You know it is

Fancy Fence
Installation at the Royal College of Art
2010

The Republic
Illustrations for The Drawer
2011

Cultures Electroni [k]
Art direction
2011
Collaboration with Nicolas Jullien
Photography by Pelle Crepin

right straight away because it comes from someone who thinks virtually the same as you as we grew and keep working together.

The bande-dessinée "Machine qui rêve" (by Tome and Janry) is also very dear to me.

What has been repeatedly used in your artwork?

Pins & Puns.

What does your work teach you?

Try not to limit myself to one medium of expression. If a creative idea is good, it should be able to work its magic on a various range of mediums: photography, illustration, clothing, film, installation, etc... It should all work as a whole, an eclectic, yet coherent whole. It's like a language used to express ideas. The words are different from one sentence to the other, but you recognize the speaker because of his "creative" accent.

Who is the No.1 leading-edge designer in your mind? Ask him/her a question.

I'd say Charlie Kaufman. He's not a graphic designer or anything like that but, as a writer, I consider him as an idea designer. And as a question, I'd like to ask him this: Do you think centuries of creativity and culture have explored everything and that ideas are just the same product with a different packaging or do you think it's possible to have a truly new and original idea?

cultures Electroni [K]

musiques, arts & technologies   www.electroni-k.org   du13 au 23 octobre 2011 — Rennes, France

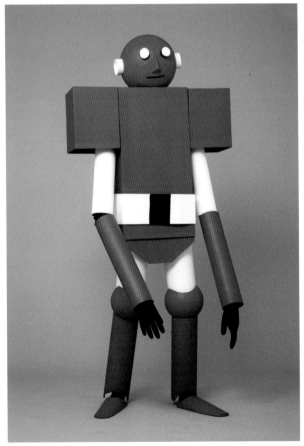

cultures Electroni [K]

musiques, arts & technologies   www.electroni-k.org   10-16 octobre 2011 — Rennes, France

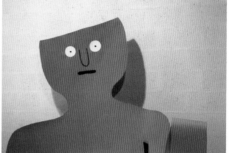

The Tourists
Solo exhibition in Nantes
2011

Machin Machine
Solo exhibition in Paris
2010

What makes you say "wooow!!" lately?
Internet.

What's the most important to you now?
Family, girlfriend, friends and my work.

Working with my brother Niwouinwouin is something quite dear to me. It's something very special to be able to work together. We're very complementary, him being a musician and me doing visuals. But we also art direct/ generate ideas together. It's very exciting to be able to work hand in hand with someone. It makes everything smooth, yet surprising and challenging.

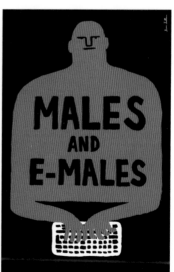

"I try not to limit myself to one medium of expression. If a creative idea is good, it should be able to work its magic on a various range of mediums: photography, illustration, clothing, film, installation, etc... It should all work as a whole, an eclectic, yet coherent whole. It's like a language used to express ideas. The words are different from one sentence to the other, but you recognize the speaker because of his 'creative' accent."

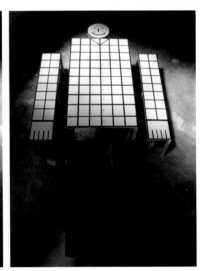

Table Man
Exhibition
2010

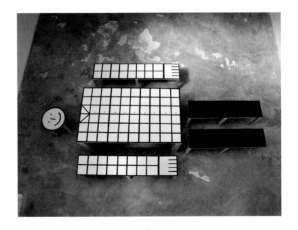

Johan Hjerpe

Johan is a brand concept developer, art director and partner of his own brand and service development agency Imaginary Life. In parallel with the strategy work Johan is highly active within the cultural field, driving projects as diverse as designing prints and fabrics for fashion, set design, magazine art direction, graphic design and concept development for various art and fashion projects.

What does your typical day look like?

I cook myself a quite ambitious breakfast and eat it. I come in a bit late. I then spend 50-70% of my day on administration and meetings. Rest of the time I use trying to figure things out and create.

parody of another, or is the same thing in a deceptive form".

What has been repeatedly used in your artwork?

Symmetry and ovals, though I try to avoid them. Personal preferences can be a prison.

Who is the No.1 leading-edge designer in your mind? Ask him/her a question.

I've come back to Stefan Sagmeister lately. For example his identity work for Casa da Musica, Portugal. I find it both explorative and to the point, connecting the building, the people working there, historic composers and contemporary events in

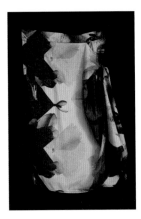

What is the wildest/craziest design practice you have done over the years?

Last year, Imaginary Life that I run with Tanya Grassley, worked on something called the Conspiracy for Good. In short, it was a pilot project with the aim to weave voluntary work into a participatory drama. Behind was Tim Kring, producer of Heroes and Nokia amongst others. Besides a lot of strategy work we did a design system built on an "unfolding grid" that enabled the participants to code messages with paper craft folding. Most of the design profile was shared hi-res, like the logo for artists and participants to use and interpret. The same elements still needed to be configurable for clear official messages. And everything needed to work online, on screen, on mobile, in print. So, wildness in the sense that it had built-in lack of control that is very unusual for design systems.

Please describe a moment/thing/person that has a strong influence on your work.

I am very inspired by two artists I work with, Goldin+Senneby. They have a way of exposing our financial reality as fiction and prove fiction to be very real. A Bataille quote that they used as title for one of their works says it well: "Each thing seen is the

What does your work teach you?

My strategic practice: to constantly redefine and understand what it is to live in an economical system such as ours. My design work: an open eye to everyday visual groupings, and sometimes the ability to understand the narrative they produce. Like:

A parked green car + rain + leaning posture + ballpoint pen =?

Plastic table + expensive Barolo wine + Blink182 + a cat =?

one visual system. My question to Mr. Sagmeister: Do you have any examples of design work connecting dimensions of a company on another axis than the visual; for example one stretching from business strategy to new modes of business relationships, or joint company/consumer transformation processes?

What makes you say "wooow!!" lately?

I just discovered a before overlooked street in Nausea by Sartre: "the city has forgotten about it. [...] There are not even murders there for lack of murderers and victims. Boulevard Noir is inhuman. Like a mineral. Like a triangle." Wow. Never before have I encountered such a strong portrait of an empty street.

What's the most important to you now?

Work wise to stay in transformation together with clients. That means to not accept because-I'm-the-client kind of directions, but also not accepting to give off-the-shelf directions - even if someone asks and pays for it. The main interest in work is to become someone else that you were not in the beginning, as someone said.

Diana Orving –
Spaces s/s 2009
Art direction/Print design
2009

Diana Orving –
Curtains s/s 2010
Art direction/Print design
2010

Diana Orving –
You a/w 2011
Art direction/Print design
2011

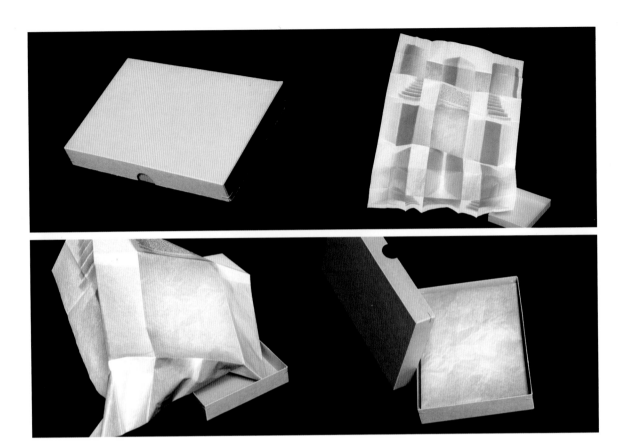

Boys Don't Cry –
Box of Untold Stories
Architect firm self-promotion
2009

The Royal University College of Fine Arts,
Stockholm – MA Exhibition
Exhibition catalogue/Visual concept
2007

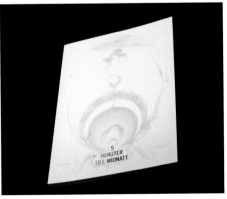

+46 Awards –
Nikoline Liv Andersen
Fashion Show
Creative direction/Set design
2007

"*Work wise to stay in transformation
together with clients.*"

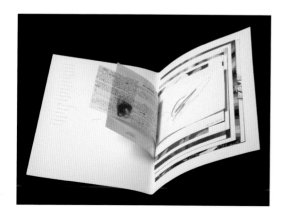

Beautiful Decay
Collage
2011

Justin Blyth

Justin Blyth is a multi-disciplinary designer, art director and artist who has been working in design, motion graphics, print, advertising, art direction and film for the better part of 10 years. Born and raised in Los Angeles, he received his BFA from Art Center in 2004 and currently lives in Amsterdam working directly with clients, agencies, and boutiques.

***Map is not Territory
(Self-initiated)***
Collage
2011

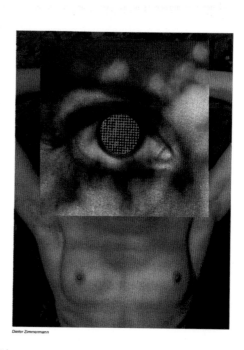

Dieter Zimmermann

179

What's your favorite part of your day?

I enjoy waking up to a cup of coffee and checking my email each morning, my creativity is usually best late at night, but I'm not gonna lie, a day outside is better than anything.

What is the wildest/craziest design practice you have done over the years?

I just directed a project where we projected an animation onto a huge building in Sydney. We made it appear that the building was burning, crumbling, exploding, filling with water, etc. That was pretty wild to see when we finally got it on

there. I also had the opportunity to live in a beautiful hotel room in Marseille last month while I designed, painted and curated the location which was really different and fun.

Please describe a moment/thing/person that has a strong influence on your work.

I take inspiration from the people and things around me. The best thing I can do for my creativity is to take a bit of time away from the computer and go outside, travel, see new places, meet people, camp in the wild, play with animals, start a fire, etc.

What has been repeatedly used in your artwork?

I'm a bit obsessed with surrealism, the occult and mysticism. I want my work to be as subjective as I can for that particular project.

What does your work teach you?

Patience, humility, confidence, self-conciousness.

Cradle of Design
Collage/Acrylic
2010

Microsoft Kin
Collage/Acrylic
2010

Who is the No.1 leading-edge designer in your mind? Ask him/her a question.

Some of my all-time favorite designs came from Push Pin Studios, the New York collective of Milton Glaser, Seymour Chwast, Reynold Ruffins, and Edward Sorel. I don't know if I have any questions for them, but I would definitely say "Thank You".

What makes you say "wooow!!" lately?

To be honest most of the things that make me say "wooow!!" aren't new. I feel wow when I see a Basquiat painting, a Native American blanket, a classic car, a pair of old boots, a crazy flower or a breathtaking landscape. I just saw the Art in the Streets show at MOCA in LA which was really inspiring. The Street Market installation is incredible.

What's the most important to you now?

My focus has really shifted over the last couple years. The most important thing to me now is taking jobs that are fun and purely creative, without having too many restrictions or bending to a rigid structure imposed by a client. I used to work just for the dollar and did a lot of uninspiring design and it really just burns me out. I love projects that break the norm, that involve travel, working outside, working with my hands, etc.

Harper Smith
Photography
Collage
2010
Collaboration with
photographer Harper
Smith

Warp Records
Package
2010

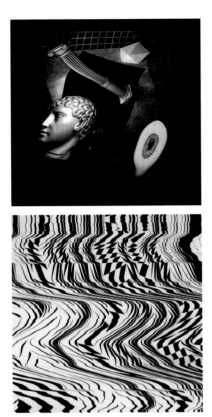

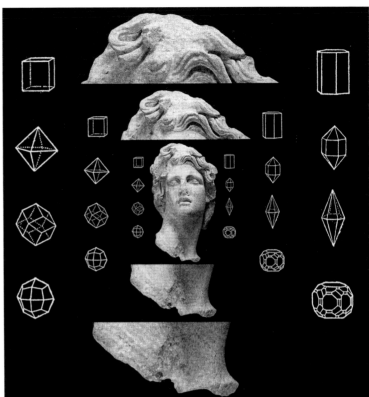

Blood is the New Black
Product
2010

*"Patience,
humility,
confidence,
self-consciousness."*

le Mystere (Self-initiated)
Collage/Acrylic
2009

Moment Skis
Product
2009

Stussy
Illustration
2009

184

1+1=3
Film/Promotional
materials/Visual
graphics at fair
2009

Kalle Hagman, the one man army designer.

1+1=3
Film/Promotional
materials/Visual graphics
at fair
2009

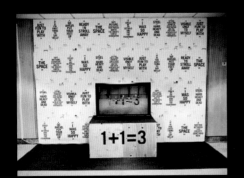

What's your favorite part of your day?

Not knowing what's gonna happen next, and always taking the unexpected road. It's easy to get into daily routines, and in some extent that can be good, but just taking another way to work, I find very rewarding.

What is the wildest/craziest design practice you have done over the years?

A lot of the craziest things I have encountered during my years as an art director and graphic designer have happened at Beckmans College of Design. Working without answering to a client opens up possibilities to do crazy stuff. In many of our projects we have been relying on sponsorship, for example, borrowing cameras, printing, working with stylists, photographers, and studios has been really rewarding to the end result. Doing 27000 posters for a furniture fair, filming in a ruin city outside Stockholm in the rain with cameras and equipment worth millions of Euros, going to Tokyo and sleeping on the floors at a friend's place together with a photographer making my end exam project, are just a portion of the weird and peculiar projects I have been working with.

Do you have any role models for your design career?

In terms of looking up to people I have always thought that it is good to have a mentor. Someone that you can talk to like a mother of your work, who understands where you're coming from and where you

Force of Attraction
Printed matter/Art direction
2009

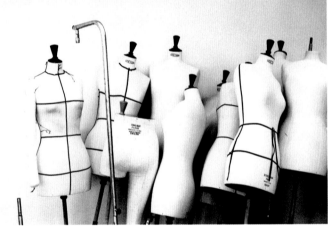

Force of Attraction
Printed matter/Art direction
2009

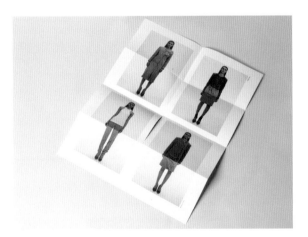

wanna go. Of course I can look at someone and think "WOW, that guy really pulled it off but that more has to do with what kind of people inspire me and that certainly does not have to do with design to do. I love to see people doing the things they love and not even question why they are doing it. It just comes natural.

What has been repeatedly used in your artwork?

I tend to come back to the same ways of working and find that when I do I'm out of ideas and have to start over again. It's usually a good thing though, to realize that you are thinking in circles. That's when I take a break, doing something completely different.

What does your work teach you?

To always question why you are doing it. I tend to forget why I'm working on a project and end up asking myself – What am I doing!? It's all about being able to see your project from afar I guess.

Who is the No.1 leading-edge designer in your mind? Ask him/her a question.

The designers that no matter how old they are never stop trying and never stop failing. That is in my mind the leading kind of designer, but not always the kind that is successful.

What makes you say "wooow!!" lately?

Moving to another country and getting to know how it is to actually live in another city. That's mind blowing and you get some impressions from it. I try to suck it all in but it's almost an overwhelming experience that I think everybody should try. That makes me say "wow!" every day.

What's the most important to you now?

Trying and seeing where the design world can take me. Who knows where I will end up next.

Force of Attraction
Printed matter/
Art direction
2009

Conceptual Paradise
Promotional poster
2008

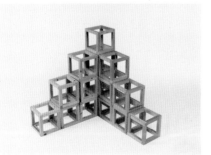

"*To always question why you are doing it. I tend to forget why I'm working on a project and end up asking myself – What am I doing!? It's all about being able to see your project from afar I guess.*"

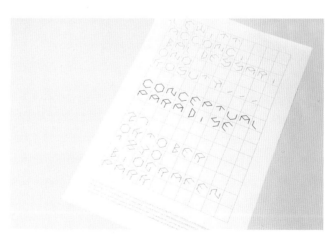

Katrin Schacke is an independent German graphic designer based in Offenbach am Main. She is working interdisciplinarily in many fields of design, including editorial and book design, photography and illustration. Her clients are different magazines like NEON, NIDO, PAGE, PRINT or T: The New York Times Style Magazine as well as the German Design Publisher Verlag Herman Schmidt Mainz. Her work was awarded several times by national and international design juries.

Parcours
Book design/Poster
2009

Katrin Schacke

Page Magazine Cover
Cover design
2010

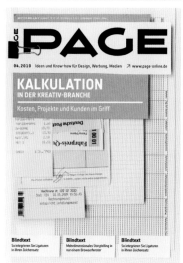

Katrin, what does your typical day look like?

Except the ritual cup of coffee every morning, I structure each day new. That's one of the good things of being a designer: the variety of tasks – from searching the first idea to whole conception and creation to realisation and production, no matter if you design a book or create an illustration series for a magazine – every job is a new challenge, with its own topics and questions. So you may have the chance to learn something new every day while dealing with different subjects and getting into content. That's fun.

What is the wildest/craziest design practice you have done over the years?

For the installations of my work "stanley – the open question magazine", which illustrates seven unsolved mysteries of science, I threw a single dart more than 350 times and tried to catch it on its fly. I stacked three orange wading pools each filled with 200 litre of milk to visualize the question of the primordial soup and the start of life on earth. I was really worried about the quality of the pools...and the horror of flooding the whole studio of my academy.For the issue "are we alone in the universe?" I generated hundreds of clouds with a fog machine. A neighbour nearly called the fire fighters because of the white smoke getting out the window every ten minutes. Fortunately everything worked well.

What has been repeatedly used in your artwork?

A repeated element in my work is the fusion of two and three dimensional spaces. Graphic shapes turn into 3D-paper-constructions to become finally again a two dimensional magazine cover. Installations and arrangements of everyday objects are three–dimensional illustrations for articles or fashion photo series. I like to use easily identifiable and well known products as metaphors for different contents. By taking them out of their ordinary context, they are getting suddenly a different meaning.

That causes irritation. It's an attempt to create unusual perspectives on abstract topics as well as making graphic design and its content more haptic.

What distinguishes your work from that of your contemporaries?

Working with 3D graphic spaces is one characteristic of my current work. But formal expressions are not the main point which distinguishes the work from designers. I think it is more about the personal attitude and

"The best part of being a designer is the chance to make the world a bit more beautiful with every work you do. You influence your cultural surroundings."

Kreativität aushalten- Psychologie für Designer
Book design
2010

the individual working process which makes the difference. Always necessary: courage, determination, and having fun as you work. Besides that it is essential for me to develop my work with regards to content. I always need a conceptual background, an idea of how to communicate a special message before I start to design. That way I try to avoid formal repetition and to create an individual design for each project. Staying unsatisfied and reflecting the own work helps to evolve it.

<u>A leading-edge designer in your mind? Ask him/her a question.</u>

What is the best strategy to inspire somebody for something he can't imagine?

<u>What is the best part of being a designer?</u>

It's the chance to make the world a bit more beautiful with every work you do. You influence your cultural surroundings.

Besides that, a designer is able to create orientation and communication. Information would stay uncommunicative without the designer's work. He structures and separates confusing complexity to clear and understandable units, gives boring but quite useful facts and delicious face. While making appetite with fascinating images he helps the reader to find an interesting access to knowledge and getting more easily into content – if that works, it is a great feeling!

<u>What would you like to be if you were not a designer?</u>

Scientist.

Mahlzeit
Fashion photo series for
NEON Magazine
2009

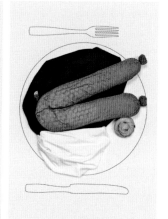

Nippon Connection Film Festival
Poster campaign
2006
Collaboration with
Alice Deußer & Jörg Baumann

Continents
Product photo series for
NIDO Magazine
2009
Collaboration with Jörg
Baumann

stanley - the open question magazine
Poster
2008

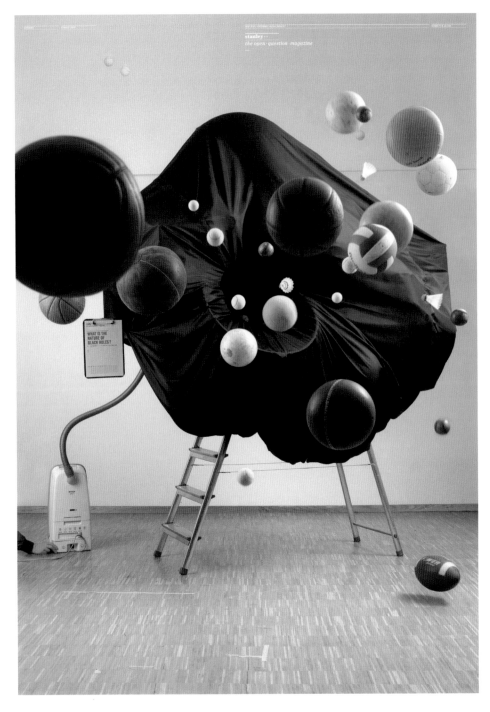

stanley - the open question magazine
Poster
2008

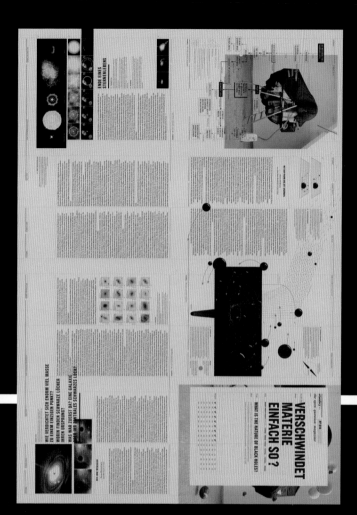

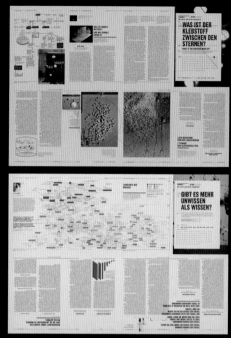

*stanley - the open
question magazine*
Poster
2008

Les Graphiquants

Les Graphiquants, graphic design studio located in Paris, consists of a creative duo formed ENSAD, a project manager and print media and a manager in communication and production. If the work order remains central to their concerns, this association allows them to self-produce and disseminate their research work. These experiments create a visual balance essential to the operation of the workshop.

2010 was a year that marked a turning point. After having invaded the French stations with their non-advertising poster, they won two European prices through the annual report of the National Contempory Arts Centre (CNAP) and the exhibition catalog of the Centre Pompidou-Metz; at the same time, they were awarded "European Agency of the Year 2011" by the European Design Awards in Vilnius.

How did you get the name Les Graphiquants?

We bent, twisted, turned and played with French language. Our name refers to a splinter group – we are 4 but sometimes much more – it is also and primarily a synthesis of the words "design" (graphisme in French), "handcraft" (artisan), "manufacture" (fabricant), "dealer" (tratiquants)...We truly love to divert, to go out of conventions and to impose over methods.

What is the wildest/craziest design practice you have done over the years?

We have designed a poster at the request of Metrobus. This poster was an order to dress billboards within Parsian subway and train stations, where no advertisement has been sold. The poster in question is a sheet of A4 paper folded then photographed and inlayed to fit the advertising space. Revenge on the graphic monopoly of advertisement mercantile communication. When the pub

is not, we are here, with an image without message, without control of intent, as the only promotion, but one step back.

What has been repeatedly used in your artwork?

We create, twist and bend the image and typography to make our design.

What distinguishes your work from that of your contemporaries?

We refuse to be categorized as part of either the communication camp or the contemporary art one. We sail in between and exploit their paradoxes - Les Graphiquants is a company organized as a collective. We try to keep a certain distance on trends. Instead we follow our own abstract way to approach the image. The purpose of our design is never obvious; we try to keep a sense of mystery in our pictures.

Who is the No.1 leading-edge designer in your mind? Ask him/her a question.

There are several graphic designers/artists that come to our mind. We like Sonia Delaunay, Frederic Teschner, the M/M and Francis Bacon. We never ask them any questions; we prefer keeping the mystery of their work.

What is the best part of being a designer?

The re-interpretation of a thought developed into image or object.

What would you like to be if you were not a designer?

The Daft Punk or a dog.

What makes you say "wooow!!" recently?

The two Delaunay's work exposed in the exhibition "Master Pieces?" at the Centre Pompidou-Metz.

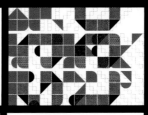

Kamchatka Gallery
Art direction
2007-2010

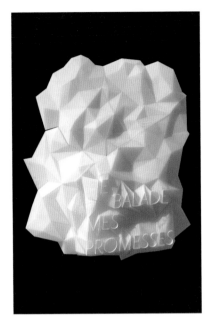

" We refuse to be categorized as part of either the communication camp or the contemporary art one. We sail in between and exploit their paradoxes – Les Graphiquants is a company organized as a collective. "

Metrobus-Floating
Poster
2009

Graphiquants
Exhibition
Exhibition
2009

Posters
Art direction
2007-2010

NAM QUIBU
EDAMQUO
SAUDIO
SAPIENTES

01

HY-
BRID
TER-
RITO
RIES

WAD Magazine
Art direction
2009

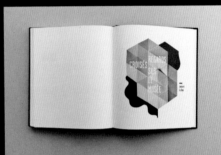

Contreversions
Edition
2009

Graphiquants
Photos – MIR-OR
Photography
2010

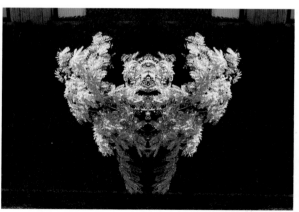

Mads Jakob Poulsen is a graphic designer from Copenhagen, Denmark. He is a senior designer at Wolff Olins, New York, where he works within identity and packaging design for major clients.

Mads' approach to design is to always base his work on a strong conceptual idea; the design should then make that idea come alive with the least amount of clutter.

This approach is his recipe for iconic and engaging design. Mads' work has received several awards internationally and he has been published in design books worldwide.

Copenhagen Parts
Visual identity/Packaging
2010

Mads Jakob
Poulsen

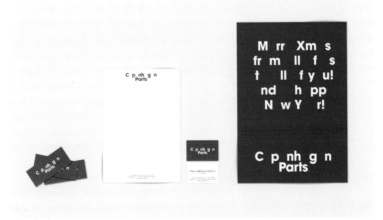

"I think the human touch to my work is very important, my style is very minimal but my work always has an extra little something, a visual joke or pun you might say."

What's your favorite part of your day?

Even though I am not a morning person it's seeing the sun in the morning on the way to work. Work wise - seeing work from yesterday with fresh eyes when I get in.

What is the wildest/craziest design practice you have done over the years?

Hmm, maybe diving into the world of professional boxing. - I did the identity for Danish World Champion boxer Mikkel Kessler so I had to do some research, I went to matches, I went to meet him and it was a look into a world I had never before been a part of.

Please describe a moment/thing/person that has a strong influence on your work.

I really think artists like Barbara Kruger for example is so inspiring. She is such a great example of sticking to one style, owning it and making it so unique and flexible at the same time.

What has been repeatedly used in your artwork?

I think the human touch to my work is very important, my style is very minimal but my work always has an extra little something, a visual joke or pun you might say.

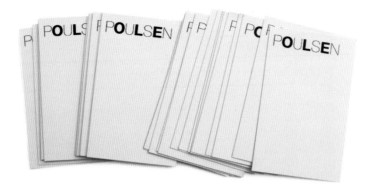

Ole Poulsen
Visual identity
2009

What does your work teach you?

To never give up.

Who is the No.1 leading-edge designer in your mind? Ask him/her a question.

These days it's becoming more and more companies and not so much individual designers creating interesting projects. However I am really inspired by Michael Bierut and the thinking that goes behind his design works. – Michael, do you want to have coffee?

What makes you say "wooow!!" lately?

When I won the Art Directors Club Young Guns Award. That was a great way to enter the design community in New York and a welcoming surprise.

What's the most important to you now?

That's a big question. Inspiration.

Ole Poulsen
Visual Identity

DDC: Se Lyset
Visual identity
2009

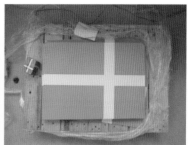

Vinyl CPH
Art direction/Conceptual
design
2010

Mark Pernice/Matic is a graphic design and illustration studio in Brooklyn, New York.

A New York native and School of Visual Arts alum, he advanced from early work in movie poster design to designing for a variety of clients and industries as a now-longtime freelance graphic designer and artist. Pernice also spent part of 2008 working under world renowned graphic designer Stefan Sagmeister and Paula Scher in 2010.

The recognition he has gotten includes the 2011 FPO Awards, Make Magazine 10 Best of 2010, HOW Magazine Outstanding Achievement award, 2009 AIGA PDA award and a Print Magazine Regional Design Annual award.

Mr. & Mrs. Mark Pernice

Mr. & Mrs. Andrew Theodorou

Mr. & Mrs. Ciro Pernice

Mrs. Carmella Tracola

Mr. & Mrs. Joseph DeCarlo

Mr. & Mrs. Zachary Smith

Mr. & Mrs. Jeffrey Charles Roberto

Doctor & Mrs. Richard Ehrlich

Mark Pernice

Mr. Ben Chan & Ms. Jennifer Eggloff

212

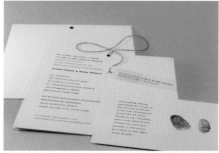

Wedding Invite
Print
2008

> " *I'm not afraid of making mistakes anymore. Having made a lot of mistakes, I'm confident in knowing that the consequences are never as bad as not taking that chance in the first place. This has given me lots of freedom.*"

What's your favorite part of your day?

There are a couple. 1. First cup of Coffee 2. When the mail comes. I still get excited to receive something that has gone on a journey through the physical world to get to me even though it's mostly junk and bills. 3. Twilight. (The time of day, not the movie.) 4. Most of all I like it when I hear from someone who has been somehow touched or at least grazed by my work.

What is the wildest/craziest design practice you have done over the years?

The Photo Booth Mask project had some pretty wild results and it was great incorporating sculpture in the design process.

The penis typography I designed for the Veer project was a fun and funny process. I had my wife sew me long beanbags stuffed with rice. I stuffed these inside my jeans to form letters that looked (hopefully) to be made from a cartoonish, large penis.

On a project about two years ago I had to photograph a model with clothespins on her nipples. By example I had to put them on my own nipples to show the model that it did not hurt too badly.

Please describe a moment/thing/person that has a strong influence on your work.

Music and playing music was very influential to me as a young designer. When I had to design my first flyer for my first band it was clear to me that I had a seamless enjoyment for doing both. When I learned that the flying pig on Pink Floyd's "Animals" album art was an elaborate balloon that became loose and rogue. It taught me that design could be really fun and pretty much lead to where I am now.

What has been repeatedly used in your artwork?

I guess there's a bit of humor in some of my work. That's arguable though.

What does your work teach you?

That I'm not afraid of making mistakes anymore. Having made a lot of mistakes, I'm confident in knowing that the consequences are never as bad as not taking that chance in the first place. This has given me lots of freedom.

Who is the No.1 leading-edge designer in your mind? Ask him/her a question.

No surprise here. Probably Stefan (Sagmeister). I'd ask him if he considered his hair his first aesthetic success.

What makes you say "wooow!!" lately?

Dark Matter. M-Theory. Nerd stuff.

What's the most important to you now?

Family, Friends, and a mental wellbeing. Doing genuine, good-natured work, which in turn keeps me genuinely interested in working.

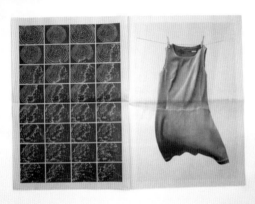

Anni Kuan Mailer
Print for Sagmeister Inc.
2008

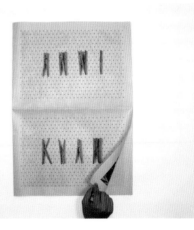

Photo Booth Mask
Self initiated
2010

ANY AM I LOOKING AT A BIG SLOPPY DISTORTED HEAD?

Apple's Photo Booth application is entry level face stretching inspiration for millions of Mac owners. In the hands of a trained professional, it's... frankly, freaking everybody out.

Mark Fenske's 'Photo Booth Mask' is the result of taking design off the page and dragging it kicking and screaming (and also drooling) into the real world. What began as an exercise to reach his in-laws how to use their iMac ended in a project that Fast Company called "almost divine grotesqueness."

"I was showing my wife's parents around their new iMac and had to show them Photo Booth. Because of course, that's the first thing you do when introducing someone to a Mac," Fenske says. "When looking back at the bizarre images, I thought it would be equally weird to see them actually in front of me."

To achieve that, he took his talented doppelganger to F/X sculptor Christian Hanson, who made Fenske's dreams come true. In latex.

"The idea was: take the 2D image that Photo Booth manipulated and create a tangible face in a real environment, then, in turn, bring it back into a 2D image," Fenske says. While 'Photo Booth Mask' may be the first in a series, there's one idea Mark is resistant to. "Using Photo Booth on the mask itself. It may create some sort of paradoxical shift where I cease to exist."

GRAPHIC DESIGN, ILLUSTRATION AND TYPOGRAPHY FOR PRINT, EDITORIAL, WEB, VIDEO, AND SO-ON.

A PARTIAL LIST OF COMPANY WE KEEP--/

Sagmeister Inc.
Virgin Mobile
Pentagram
Lincoln Center for the Performing Arts
Mtv
Inasound.com
Grill Team Media
Moto Records
CMJ Music Monthly
Loudmouth Inc.
Barnes Coy Architects
CityVet
The Luminaire / 3000
Voxel dot net
WJAM records
The Tennesseean
Canopy Verde Handbags
Weathervane Music Group

YOU MIGHT HAVE SEEN US-------------/

Print Magazine
How Magazine
Clear Magazine Cover Issue 14
Graphic Poster Annual 2010
100% More Graphic Elements
Rockport Press
Liaoning Science and Technology

Mark Fenske
Matic Design
need some design?nl: mark@maticart.com
sending a love letter?: theart@maticart.com
office: 347-987-2845
mobile: 516-355-0438

62 Monitor St.
Unit 3B
Brooklyn, NY 11222

www.maticart.com
www.markfenske.com

YOU MIGHT HAVE READ ABOUT US-------/

Wired
The Huffington Post
Fast Company
Gizmodo
Sundance Channel
Designboom
Make Magazine
The Atlantic - Andrew Sullivan
Boinoboing
Today and Tomorrow
Wooster Collective
Buzzfeed
Gizmodo
Gearfuse
Designevolution
The Strange Attractor
1MCe
Neatorama
Urlesque

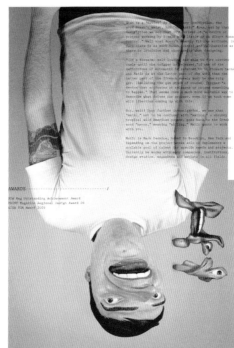

What is a Designer? By dictionary description, one who "plans, works, inventions or creates." Keep, and by that definition we are. But it's a pretty short entre-to-process working by itself without all the silver Roman numerals. "Well when Noun's Weekly fit the arthouse, In fact there is so much-Noun, noun-ing, and deliberating as there is intuition and choreography when designing.

"It's a firearm: self loaded and able to fire certain rounds until the trigger is released. "If one of the definitions of automatic we referred to is firearm terms and facts is at the latter part of the word than the farther part of the firearm surely must be the very gun. (Reloading the gun ahead of course) Trigger "a device that activates or releases or causes something to happen." That seems like a much more suitable way to describe what solves our purpose, even if we took some willibertine coming up with this.

Ho! wait! Down further (Investigation), we see that "matic," not to be confused with "medium," a shrubby tropical wild American pepper, goes back to the Greek word "matos," meaning "willing." Matic wants to work with you.

Matic is Mark Fenske, based in Brooklyn, New York and depending on the project draws into an homeowners a scalable pool of talent for specific needs and projects. Currently he works with many companies, institutions, design studios, magazines and authors, in all fields.

AWARDS-------------------------------/

How Mag Outstanding Achievement Award
PRINT Magazine Regional Design Award 06
AIGA XOR Award 2005

Mark Fenske
Matic Design
62 Monitor St.
Unit 3B
Brooklyn, NY 11222

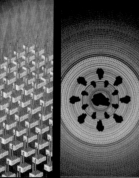

***Darwin ChairQuestion
Magazine***
Design/Illustration for
Sagmeister Inc.
2010

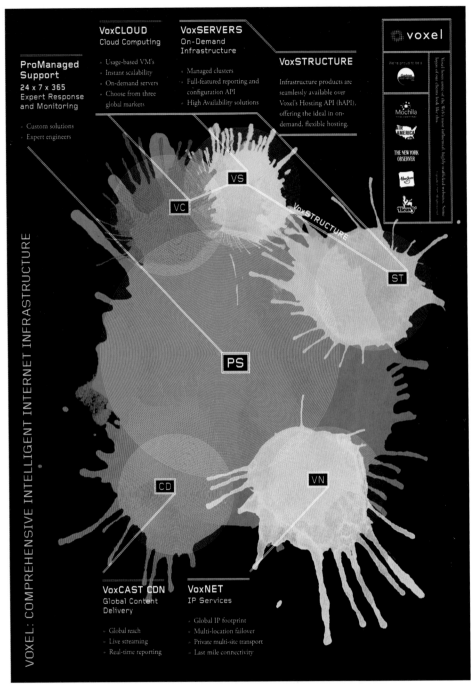

voxel

We're proud to be a

Gawker
MEDIA

Mochila

THE
AMERICA
LIST

THE NEW YORK
OBSERVER

Heavy

Voxel hosts some of the Web's most influential, highly-trafficked websites. Some logos of our clients look like this.

VoxCLOUD
Cloud Computing

» Usage-based VM's
» Instant scalability
» On-demand servers
» Choose from three
  global markets

VoxSERVERS
On-Demand
Infrastructure

» Managed clusters
» Full-featured reporting and
  configuration API
» High Availability solutions

VoxSTRUCTURE

Infrastructure products are
seamlessly available over
Voxel's Hosting API (hAPI),
offering the ideal in on-
demand, flexible hosting.

**ProManaged
Support**
24 x 7 x 365
Expert Response
and Monitoring

» Custom solutions
» Expert engineers

VS

VC

VoxSTRUCTURE

ST

PS

CD

VN

VoxCAST CDN
Global Content
Delivery

» Global reach
» Live streaming
» Real-time reporting

VoxNET
IP Services

» Global IP footprint
» Multi-location failover
» Private multi-site transport
» Last mile connectivity

VOXEL: COMPREHENSIVE INTELLIGENT INTERNET INFRASTRUCTURE

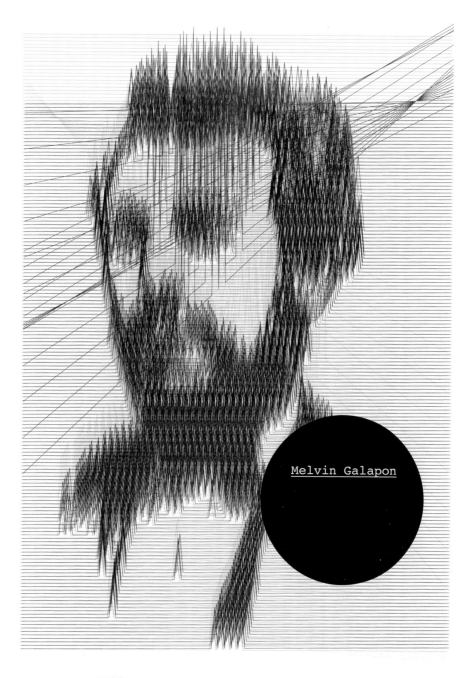

Melvin Galapon

Illustrator and designer Melvin Galapon was born in the South of England in 1981, yet hails from Burnley, a small town in the Northwest of England. He is a graduate from Central St. Martin's. His prolific output has seen him work with Wallpaper*, The New York Times, The Guardian & Howies to name but a few and he has been featured in various magazines worldwide.

Galapon is currently based in London where he works on a mix of illustrations, installations and design work.

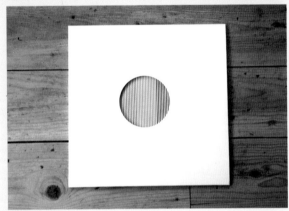

Show Off Record
Packaging/Art direction
2008
Photography by Anne-Cecile Caillaud

Reception Series (Self-Initiated)
Graphical patterns
2010

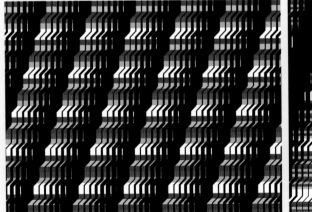
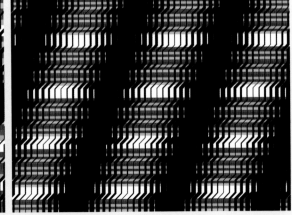

Glitch Installation
Set design
2010

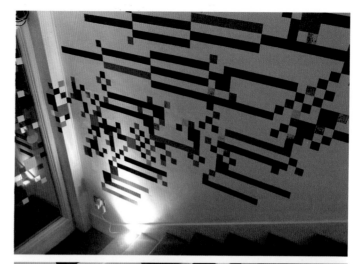

What is the wildest/craziest design practice you have done over the years?

I got asked to create a portrait of comic writer Alan Moore for a friend's magazine and I wanted to try a new technique. I always liked the idea of making a portrait out of coloured pencils in some way and spend some time working out the best way to do it. I eventually settled on using the pencil shavings to build up the portrait which proved to be great fun.

What has been repeatedly used in your artwork?

Pixels, lines, dots, type, vinyl and shapes are all recurring elements.

What distinguishes your work from that of your contemporaries?

I guess my interests, the way, I think/ analyze things and the materials I use separate me from other designers.

A leading-edge designer in your mind? Ask him/her a question.

What music do you like working to?

What is the best part of being a designer?

Getting paid to do what I love doing!

What would you like to be if you were not a designer?

A guitarist in an electro/indie band.

What makes you say "wooow!!" lately?

I went to Tokyo for the first time very recently and that really makes me go "woooow!!" I just love the vibe of the city; everyone I met was really cool and really friendly. I'm looking forward to going back there again at some point!

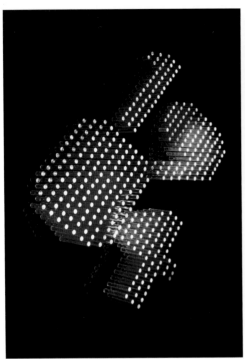

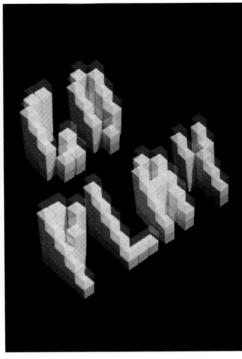

(Left)
Wired US 19.04
Typographic
illustration
2011

(Right)
ESPN
Illustration
2011

AV
Typographic illustration
2010

*"I guess my interests, the way,
I think/analyze things and the
materials I use separate me from
other designers."*

Creative Review Portrait
One of a series of portraits
2010

The Future is Now
Typographic illustration
2010

**Love is Blind
(Self-Initiated)**
Legibility typographic
experiment
2009

New
Typographic illustration
2011

more+ studio

more+ studio was established in Wuxi
and Beijing by Juanjuan Long and Erxu
Chen, 2010. They work as a flexible system
of "2+n", widely collaborating with
people from different backgrounds and
creating design in multiple forms. So far
they specialize in space design, branding,
orientation systems, product design, digital
media and printing.

What's your favorite part of your day?

The time when we say good night.

What is the wildest/craziest design practice you have done over the years?

We once worked on a project about presenting a city by an information system. In order to realize the abstract things, we created some icons such as a flower, a stack of stone or a cloud to carry out the information of a city.

Please describe a moment/thing/person that has a strong influence on your work.

When I saw the poster of Paul Rand in my high school, I was impressed by the power of design. My impulse of design was provoked for the first time.

What has been repeatedly used in your artwork?

"Possiblity." We are always trying to keep some leeway in design, providing our artwork with openness.

What does your work teach you?

Catch the shy little bird called chance.

Who is the No.1 leading-edge designer in your mind? Ask him/her a question.

My mother. I can still remember the year when I graduated, I saw her making a mobile phone bag for me. The pattern (my animal of Chinese zodiac), the fonts (my name), the cloth and colors of the thread she picked, mix and match together to be something purely harmonious and exquisite. I learned those skills when I became a design student, but without any design education background, she seems well perceived a design system on her own, amazing isn't it?

What makes you say "wooow!!" lately?

Six-piece burr puzzle. It is said that the six-piece burr puzzle was made by a famous Chinese craftman Luban, for his son. The puzzle has a simple yet complicated structure that can be solved in hundreds of ways.

What's the most important to you now?

Slow down.

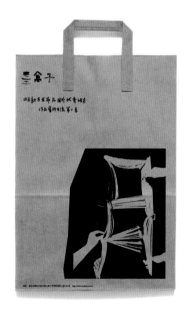

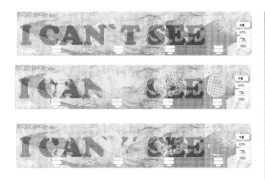

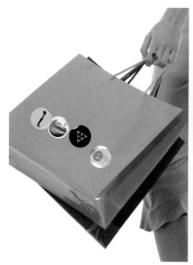

"Catch the shy little bird called chance."

Floating wall
Environmental graphics
2009

MyORB

MyORB is an art + design practice based in New York City, established by Lucie Kim. Their projects vary from commissioned pieces such as identities, websites, posters, animations and illustrations to an output of self-published work. They work spans across various platforms such as interactive, but also includes installations and workshops. They aim for their work to be curious, intriguing and playful.

What does your typical day look like?

I get to the studio between 9 am and 9:30 am. I catch up on emails and get in touch with clients. Between 10:15 am and noon I try to concentrate on production work, such as getting files ready for printers or dealing with developers. After lunch I concentrate on creative and conceptual work. In the late afternoon I meet with designers and discuss projects and designs. Most of the time, the day ends at 7 pm. Maybe once or twice a week I stay past 9 pm for a deadline or to write a proposal.

What is the wildest/craziest design practice you have done over the years?

Right now we are trying to create ice sculptures and photograph them for a project.

Maybe it does not constitute as crazy, but it is very challenging.

Please describe a moment/thing/person that has a strong influence on your work.

The strongest influences are the people closest to me. I respect my designer husband/friend's opinions. In fact their feedback is very important to me. I also look to art for inspiration. But in general I think life is what inspires me the most. I think it is important to travel and experience different cultures.

What has been repeatedly used in your artwork?

Humor. Not all the work we produce is funny, but I think many projects and especially the self-initiated ones are quite quirky – in my opinion at least.

What does your work teach you?

My work teaches me to be modest. Even after years of experience and working with clients, I am repeatedly confronted with new and unforeseen situations. I keep on learning and constantly have to re-evaluate my thinking and approach. Not only in terms of design and new technology, but also in terms of history, business, law and finance. Running a studio is a challenge day in and day out.

Who is the No.1 leading-edge designer in your mind? Ask him/her a question.

Alexander McQueen. - Why?

What makes you say "wooow!!" lately?

I just spent 5 days in Hawaii. The vegetation is unbelievable. I saw a bird of paradise plant that can grow as high as 30 feet. It looks amazing! Nature offers the most fantastic visual wonders.

What's the most important to you now?

My Family.

Hail to the pencil
Product
2011

Cause & Effect
VI
2009

Mind Trip
Animation
2009

Martin Friedrich
Creative direction/
Illustration/Animation
2009

Black Umbrella
Branding
2009

SHIZOPHRENIA

—

ΛBⅭDEFGHIJ𝖱LM
NOPQRSTUVWXYZ

ΛbⅭⅾℰℱHKM
RUWXyZ

1234557580

Λ TYPEFΛⅭE By MyORB

"My work teaches me to be modest. Even after years of experience and working with clients, I am repeatedly confronted with new and unforeseen situations. I keep on learning and constantly have to re-evaluate my thinking and approach. Not only in terms of design and new technology, but also in terms of history, business, law and finance. Running a studio is a challenge day in and day out."

Schizophrenia Typeface
Typeface
2009

The 341
VI
2009

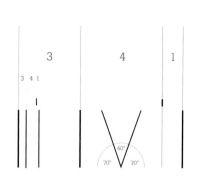

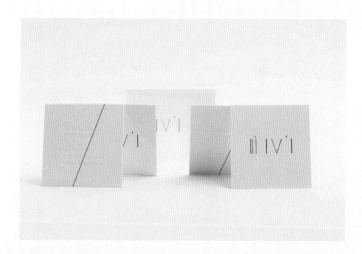

Martin Friedrich
Creative direction/
Illustration/Animation
2009

Nam

Brazil#1
Self artwork
2007

"Rather than 'what' to use as materials, I am more interested in 'how' to use the materials."

Nam is an artist group originally established by Nakazawa Takayuki (graphic designer) and Manaka Hiroshi (photographer).

Currently, over ten artists from various backgrounds belong to Nam, searching for the possibilities in the world of visual arts based on their theme, "A fantasy in life".

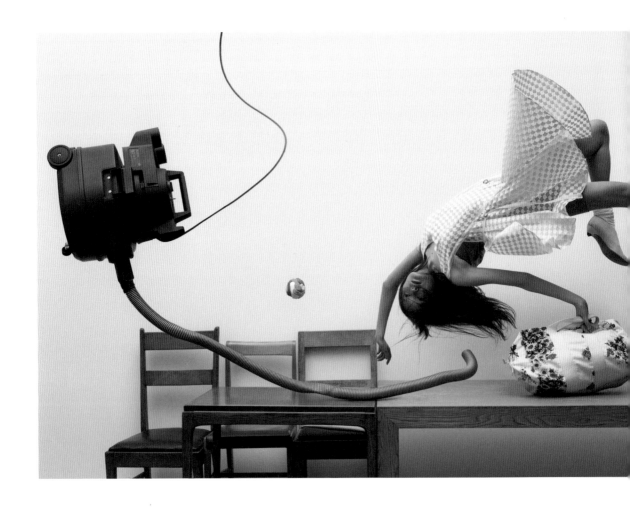

How did you get the name Nam?

It is just a wordplay but there is a similar sound in Japanese prayer.

What is the wildest/craziest design practice you have done over the years?

The image called "Panic Room". It was created by hanging every object in the room with silken guts, under the concept of making a room rotated by 180 degrees.

What has been repeatedly used in your artwork?

We often create images using materials at hand as much as possible. One of the reasons is because we are low budget. Rather than "what" to use as materials, I am more interested in "how" to use the materials.

What distinguishes your work from that of your contemporaries?

When I work as Nam, I am consciously trying to find a different methodology rather then following the royal road or establish ways of expression.

A leading-edge designer in your mind? Ask him/her a question.

I cannot specify because there are so many. I like designers who provocatively present new sense of value. What I'd love to ask them is "do you get anxious when you are about to present the world with a new sense of value, which had never existed before? Are you aware 100% in the process of production that what you are trying to do is new?"

What is the best part of being a designer?

That I can realize what I thought and visualized.

FallRoom
Self artwork
2007

<u>Tell me, what would you like to be if you
were not a designer?</u>

I like simply handwork so it could be nice to
live as an artisan of traditional handicrafts.

<u>What makes you say "wooow!!" lately?</u>

The film by Alexander N. Sokurov "Russian
Ark".

Kotaro Isaka Book "sos no saru"
Book cover
2009

blanc. Album "canvas"
CD artwork
2009

Neo 2 Magazine
Editorial
2009

Outside of Screen
Self artwork
2007

Twilight
Galaxy
METRIC

EN ESTAS PÁGINAS TE MOSTRAMOS EL
TRABAJO QUE EL COLECTIVO CREATIVO
JAPONÉS NAM HA REALIZADO PARA
NEO2. EN LAS ÚLTIMAS PÁGINAS
INCLUIMOS UNA ENTREVISTA CON SUS
DOS FUNDADORES.

Artwork: Nam < www.n-a-m.org >
Dirección de arte: TAKAFUMI WAKAZAWA
Fotógrafo: HIROSHI MANAKA
Entrevista: JAVIER ABIO

NUESTRO CONCEPTO ES "FANTASÍA EN LA VIDA". PODRÍAMOS DECIR QUE LA REGLA PRINCIPAL ES EXPERIMENTAR.

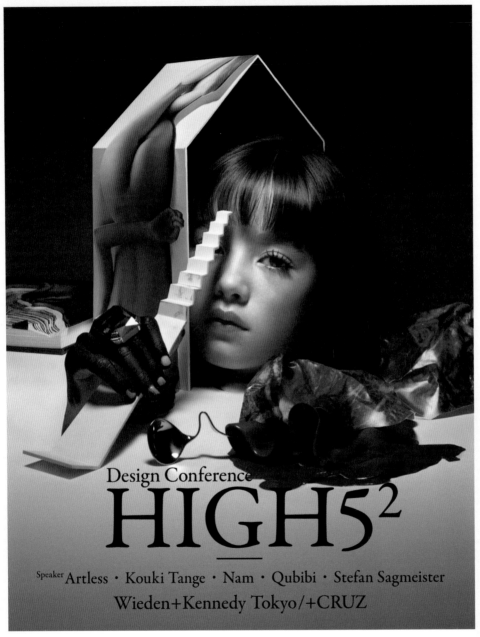

Oh Yeah studio is a duo, Christina Magnussen and Hans Christian Øren. The studio has had a natural development from a hobby into a multi-disciplinary design studio with two full-time designers. We're still in our second year of establishment. We met in school where we started collaborating and doing our own "thing". We wanted to make idealistic projects and explore new fields and have fun. We started out just "doing after dinner" which is a symbol of being creative besides (paid) work, where you work against deadlines and find little time to explore.

She Runs Like an Animal in the Sky (Self-Initiated)
Illustration
2010

Oh Yeah Studio

How did you get the name Oh Yeah Studio?

When we started working as designers in Norway, the freedom we had as students quickly ended. So we formed Oh Yeah Studio to have a place or a platform where we still could do projects on our own premises.

Most of the works we have done are something we just had to do. Oh Yeah Studio is for inspiration, play and a place to grow, so the name had to have a positive sound to it, like "Awesome!" or "Oh yeah!" We started out back in 2007, but it was not until 2009 that we got serious about it.

What is the wildest/craziest design practice you have done over the years?

That would be the time we had a project where we had to explore the difference between pornography and eroticism.

When you see a naked person in a picture, is that pornography or eroticism, and if it is porn – when/where do you draw the line? So, we asked two models (life drawing) to be a part of our project. We got a room at the finest hotel in Oslo, Grand Hotel, and asked the models to act out/jump around on the sofa, the chairs, on tables, etc. It was fun!!

Whaleless
Art project
2008

Beautiful Decay
Illustration/
Typography
2008

Computer Arts
Typography/
Editorial
2009

What has been repeatedly used in your artwork?

It depends on the project and we are always going for something new, but I have to say that geometric shapes are a big thing with us. We do try not to use the same objects/forms in all illustrations, but sometimes it just fits. So we use it.

We try not to think too much about this. It's more important that we have made something we are satisfied with, and pushed ourselves forward.

Abstract shapes, drawing mixed with vector, nature, people/portraits and animals seem often to be presented in our images. We try to move this in new directions.

What distinguishes your work from that of your contemporaries?

I guess we have a quite illustrative design expression that is made up often from the hand drawn. This, with a repeated use of geometric shapes, forms a visual language which, after a prelude, can distinguish us from another designers.

A leading-edge designer in your mind? Ask him/her a question.

MVM, aka Magnus Voll Mathiassen is a great Norwegian designer with a strong and interesting visual voice, always pushing things forward.

HI-FI klubben
Editorial/
Illustration
2010
Collaboration with
Gazette design
agency

Sirens and Us
Sleeve design
2009
Designed by Hans when
working at Norwegian Ink;
Collaborated with Frode
Nordbø.

SPANSKE KONGENS FAVORITT

À få perfekt i eget land er som kjent vanskelig. Lite er det muligens enklere, og Jan Pettersen, administrerande direktør i Bodegas Rey Fernando de Castilla, er mer kjent i Spania enn i Norge. Når Kong Juan Carlos inviterer til fest er det ofte produkter fra Pettersen i glassene. Nå vil han også bli mer kjent i Norge.

Alt uten gullslegging har Jan Pettersen vært interesert i god mat og drikke. Mens andre tjueåringar drakk øl sommersesen, traddig unge Pettersen sommeresein hos Rey Fernando de Castilla.

BRANDY OG SHERRY Mens Pettersen arbeidet med sin mustergrad i bacelona, banket Osborne på døren. De ønsket nordmannen som maltere. Arbeidet med forkeptamerte produkter ga mermosk, og etter hvert kunne Jan Pettersen smykke seg med tittelen administrerande direktør for internasjonal aktivitet i Europa.

– Jeg var med på hele utviklingen av Osborne from la den unike proteljamen rislasspot har i dag, i fortold til spansk mat- og drikkekultur, sier Pettersen.

Mot slutten av forrige århusen ville Osborne legge ned aathereiskopet Duff Gordon etter nye utfordringar, og ønsket å kjøpe selskapet. Gothe ferte til dårvejnen i tankebedillen Osborne, og det endte med at de ville beholde merkert selv.

FERNANDO DE CASTILLA Jan Pettersen hadde etter hvert slått et kjent navn i spanske brandy- og sherryketter, og mens han diskuterte kjøp av Duff Gordon, kom han også i kontakt med eierne av Bodegas Rey Fernando de Castilla. Kontakt ble til avtale, og i 2000 kjøpte Pettersen bodegaen sammen noen partnere, i dag eier Jan Pettersen sammen med andre norske interesser 70 prosent i selskapet. Merkenannet Rey Fernando de Castilla ble best etablert i 1968, men historien går tilbake til 1837 da familien Andrada-Vanderwilde startet med kommersiell produksjon og salg av vin i Jerez-distriktet.

– Beholdningen besto av gran reserva brandy, gammel sherry bassel på peder almdmesduon og gammel og eksklusiv rhenyedrok. Den første utfordringen var å internasjonalisere merkevaren Fernando de Castilla siden 95 prosent av salget var innenlands, fortelte Pettersen.

Q: How are you, Magnus?
A: I am doing just fine, though I am very hungry and the water has been temporarily shut down there. No coffee or toilet for us in the nearest future.

What is the best part of being a designer?

Be creative, to express yourself and the diversity of it all – every project is different and you always learn new things. I go to work thinking: today I'm going to make something new and interesting.

What would you like to be if you were not a designer?

Hans: I think I would be an architect, a photographer or an inventor. I would also like to work in the Red Cross or similar organizations.

Christina: Would probably work in National Geographic and/or with animals on some level.

What makes you say "wooow!!" recently?

The work of Justin Maller, Mash design, Hvass&Hannibal and I am Pelle.

BAR magazine
Editorial/
Illustration
2009-2010

BAREN SOM LABORATRIUM

FREMTIDENS COCKTAIL ER HER. PÅ TAILOR I
NEW YORK BLANDER UREN FREEMAN DRINKER MED
BACONFETT, TYGGIS OG PUFFET RIS.

LIVET ETTER BARDØ······DEN

HVA SKJER MED EN BAR NÅR SKJEBNEN BESTEMMER AT DEN
IKKE LENGER KAN DRIVES?

Oh Yeah Studio
(Self-Initiated)
Poster
2010

OH YEAH STUDIO 2010

*"Be creative,
to express
yourself and the
diversity of it all
— every project
is different and
you always
learn new
things. I go to
work thinking:
today I'm
going to make
something new
and interesting."*

MTV Feeler
Art direction
2009

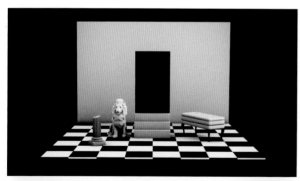

Pablo Alfieri is a graphic designer and illustrator born in 1982 in Buenos Aires, Argentina. In 2002 he entered the program of Graphic design in U.B.A. (University of Buenos Aires) and discovered his passion for design, illustration and typography.

Since 2006 he has been working in Design Studios like RDYA Design Group and Punga Visual Consorcio, and in January of 2008 he created "Playful", a showcase of his personal works, a free space where he plays and has fun with colors, typography and geometry shapes, and the basis of his creative work. Recently Playful has joined Gula, to create Plenty, one of the most important studios in Argentina in motion graphics and design.

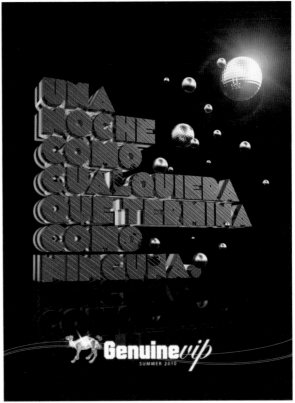

Happy August
Typography
2009

Camel
Magazine ads
2009

Pablo, what does your typical day look like?

I wake up pretty early, have a Mate (typical Argentine beverage, you can Google it!) and then go to work (not without arguing with half of the lousy drivers I meet!) I work with 7 people that I drive crazy most of the time, but they like me anyway! At least until I beat them on the PlayStation. And then I go back home to chill out with my girl. Not very crazy, but is my life, and I like it!

What is the wildest/craziest design practice you have done over the years?

Right now we are working for MTV on a very rewarding project, since they let us do whatever we wanted to. And when you do whatever you want it's always great fun!

What has been repeatedly used in your artwork?

I used stars and lights in every project for a long time. If someone dares to ask me for a star ever again I'll kill them!

What distinguishes your work from that of your contemporaries?

I do strong work on typography. I love the possibilities I have with it.

A leading-edge designer in your mind? Ask him/her a question.

To Rodchenko, I'd ask what was he thinking when doing most of his designs; and to Stefan Sagmeister, I'd ask if he wants to work with me.

Happy 2010 (Self-Initiated)
Set design
2009

"I do strong work on typography. I love the possibilities I have with it."

What is the best part of being a designer?
To have fun doing what I love. And make
money out of it!

What would you like to be if you were not
a designer?
I'd probably be a chef, or I'd have a
restaurant. I love food, I love eating!

What makes you say "wooow!!" recently?
The possibilities ahead of me, and my new
Iphone!

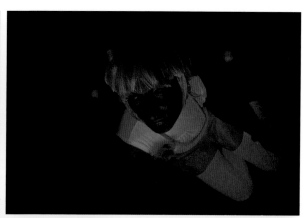

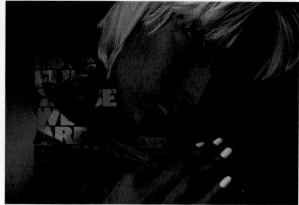

Play & Fluo
(Self-Initiated)
2010

Pam & Jenny

"To create and to learn new things everyday."

Founded by Nathalie Pollet (after leading the Designlab studio from 1998 until 2009), Pam & Jenny is a creative and pragmatic graphic studio born from the wish to preserve flexibility and the capability to fulfill all his missions armed with expertise.

Based in Brussels, Pam & Jenny keeps long term privileged relations with clients from the private and cultural sectors in Belgium and France. Depending on the needs, the studio advises and organizes visual identities, images and illustrations, books, websites and signage.

Nathalie, how did you get the studio name Pam&Jenny?

MY DOG'S NAME IS PAMELA
MY CAT'S NAME IS JENNIFER

What has been repeatedly used in your artwork?

REPEATING IS BORING

What is the wildest/craziest design practice you have done over the years?

A 600 METER LONG
ILLUSTRATION

What distinguishes your work from that of your contemporaries?

YOU TELL ME

A leading-edge designer in your mind? Ask him/her a question.

WHAT DISTINGUISHES YOUR
WORK FROM MINE?

What is the best part of being a designer?

TO CREATE AND TO LEARN
NEW THINGS EVERYDAY

What would you like to be if you were not a designer?

A ROCK STAR

What makes you say "wooow!!" lately?

THAT JAPANESE FOOD I ATE
YESTERDAY

Eric Beauduin
Graphic design
2008-2010

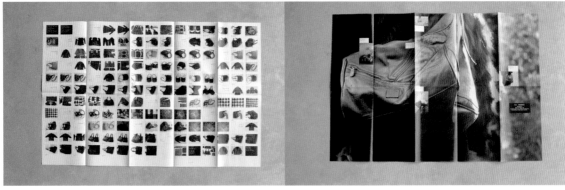

Jean-Paul Knott
Graphic design
2010

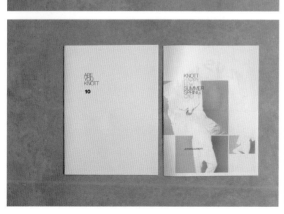

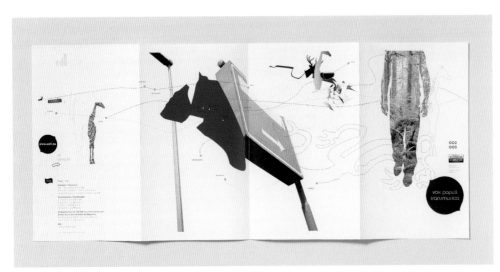

258

Netwerk
Identity/
Graphic design
2003

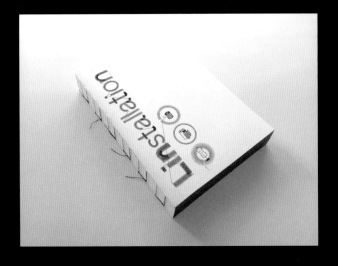

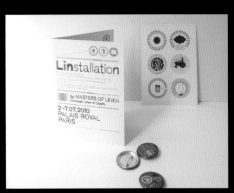

**CELC – European
Confederation of Linen and
Hemp**
Identity/Illustration
2009-2010

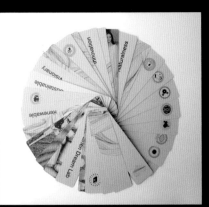

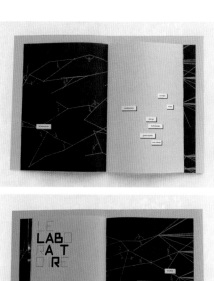

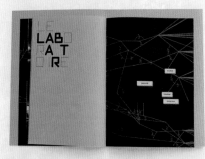

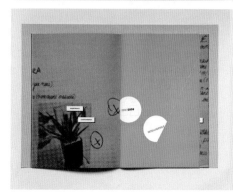

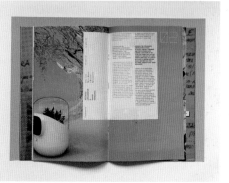

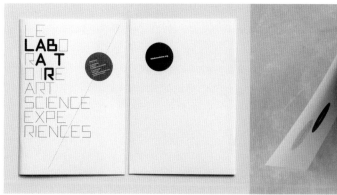

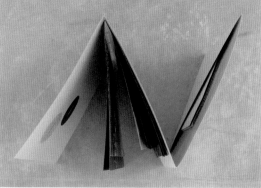

KUNSTSTOF(F)
Identity/Book design
2007

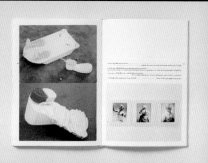

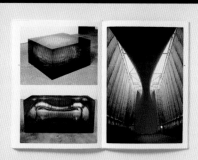

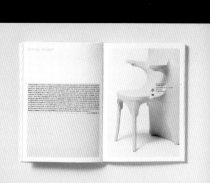

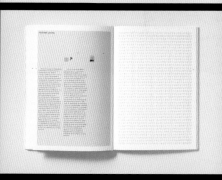

SOFAM
Graphic design/Illustration
2009

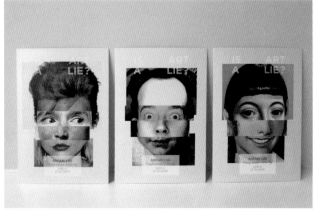

PMKFA

What's your favorite part of your day?

When I bike home from the office, it's a moment of relaxation and thoughts with a different distance and perspective. Many ideas come up on these rides. Sometimes I meet up with my girlfriend and bike with her and it's really a good moment.

What is the wildest/craziest design practice you have done over the years?

When I did the Probarious exhibition. It was late Nov and Dec and all the stuff was built and assembled in an outdoor workshop between Tokyo and Yokohama. I started working around 8 in the morning and left when it was too dark and cold to continue at night. I cut myself several times with the blade but because my hands were covered in plastic glue no blood could seep out. Some local alcoholics came by and held shows like only alcoholics can. It was both really weird and interesting, especially as Tokyo often can feel all posh and shiny so it was a good reminder of all the slightly trashier and gritty areas that inner city people tend to forget about.

Please describe a moment/thing/person that has a strong influence on your work.

That's a hard one. I have no one that I follow very closely anymore and my music taste is more fragmented than ever but maybe I could say that the band Salem is inspiring in terms of energy. I work hard to come across those moments when you feel that you've tried and managed to do something new, that's what PMKFA is all about and I treasure and hunt those moments.

Graphic designer PMKFA is now residing in Tokyo after half a decade in Copenhagen and London. His work spans different disciplines such as music graphics, the fashion industry and three dimensional art installations.

His colorful and often psychedelic work has been created for clients such as Adidas, Sixpack France, DC Shoes, Uniqlo, Nudie jeans, Wesc, Junior Senior and Lo-Fi-Fnk. Since 2006 he's also the art-director of his co-founded clothing label It's Our Thing.

Probarious Exhibition
Installation design
2008

What has been repeatedly used in your artwork?

My main tool is obviously the computer but I look at it as a tool that can be used to develop craftsmanship as any analogue tool and I try to find my own ways to get around inside the tool. I try to add an analogue-esque x-factor in there, something I work a lot with when I use photography and paint work. I used to have elements coming back in the past, but not anymore, maybe there are subtle feelings coming back, but I leave that to the viewer to conclude.

What does your work teach you?

Discipline, happiness, that I should work more with my business manager to add another 0 to the invoices, that with will and dedication you can get very far and that I've found what I wanna work with for the rest of my life.

Who is the No.1 leading-edge designer in your mind? Ask him/her a question.

I have none. Maybe Shigeo Fukuda but unfortunately he passed away in early 2009. Rest in peace Fukuda sensei.

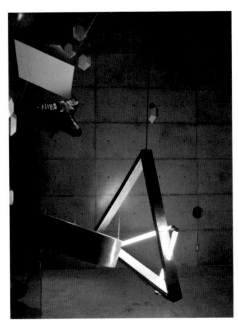

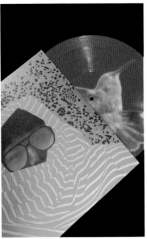

Sixpack France "Galaxy" Series
Fashion/Textile design
2008

Stuffa & Andy Feat. Mapei – "Pretty Girls"
Graphic design/ Packaging design
2008

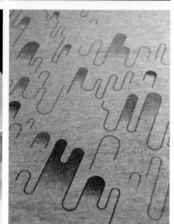

What makes you say "wooow!!" lately?

The track "King Night" by Salem, visiting Beijing, certain clients' disorganization, my nephew's first crawling "steps", Anish Kapoor and Georgian food.

What's the most important to you now?

To find new directions. Something I will spend the rest of the year to define. To get into filming and photographing more, to art-direct more and get back on working on larger projects. But first I will have some well deserved vacation as I've worked the whole summer.

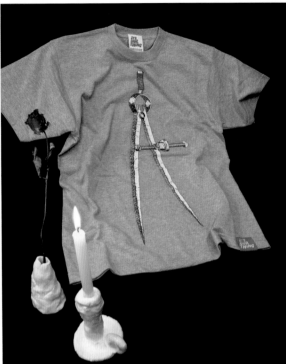

It's Our Thing Presents DJ
Seep in "2079"
Graphic design/Packaging design
2009

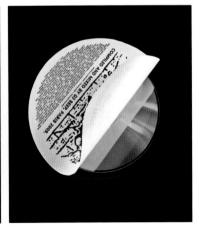

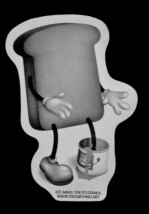

Sixpack & DC Shoes
Fashion/Graphic design/Packaging design
2009

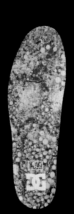

"Discipline, happiness, that I should work more with my business manager to add another 0 to the invoices, that with will and dedication you can get very far and that I've found what I wanna work with for the rest of my life."

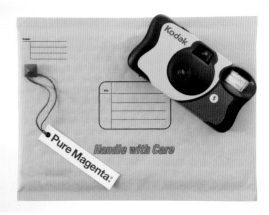

Pure Magenta is Sarah Kissell, a graphic
designer and graduate of the Minneapolis
College of Art + Design.

What distinguishes your work from that of your contemporaries?

What does your typical day look like?

- ■ Thinking about Designing
- □ Coffee
- ■ Designing

What would you like to be if you were not a designer?

"What's the best thing you've ever been asked?"

What has been repeatedly used in your artwork?

What is the wildest/craziest design practice you have done over the years?

What is the best part of being a designer?

Seeing people interact with things you make.

A leading-edge designer in your mind? Ask him/her a question.

What's the best thing you've ever been asked?

What makes you say "wooow!!" lately?

The internet, and probably will be for quite some time.

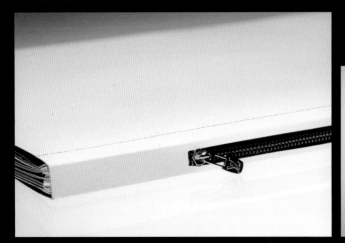

*Faux Real: The Black Market
of Counterfeit Luxury*
Exhibition Catalog
2008

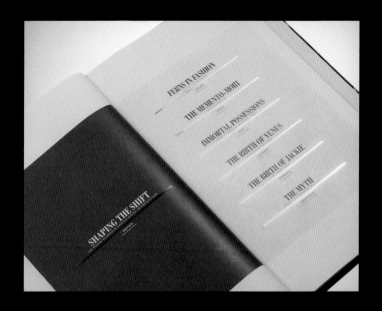

***Still Remains: The Immortal
Cycle of an Icon, Jacqueline
Kennedy Onassis***
Body bag/Exhibition catalog
2008

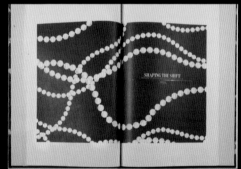

There is nothing simple about the roles that photographic images play in our collective lives: they
are, in essence, the backbone of our socialization
process, and they communicate to us through a variety
of means, channels, forms and functions that may
be both paradoxical and contradictory. They create
our cultural mythologies and standards of beauty—
and then, following the whims of fashion and novelty
in our society, continuously destroy and replace them.

But it is today, nearly fifty years later, that within
the vivid vernacular of November 22, 1963 we see a
photographic transformation—from fragmented stills
into a verbally metaphoric, visually continuous system:
a moment where the instincts of the First Lady shaped
the shift in one of the most defining events in American
history. A moment that blossomed into something
much greater than what her image could capture:
She symbolized an end as well as a beginning—
She signified renewal as well as change.

What remains is a fragrant preservation of her message:
A message to our instincts, to our self awareness, to our
national identity—What does it mean to be American?
What ingredients will make up the truest myth?

**Still Remains: The Immortal Cycle of
an Icon, Jacqueline Kennedy Onassis**
Body Bag/Exhibition Catalog
2008

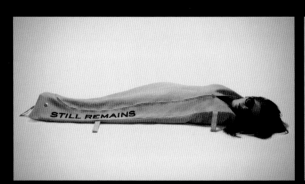

PUNK ROCK

Extreme Noise
Identity system/Process book
2007

Raquel Quevedo

"Have fun with responsibility. Be open-minded as a child with a work purpose. Be creative without boundaries."

**Refranes Visuales–
Saying, visual objects
(Self-initiated)**
Art direction/Exhibition/
Product
2009

Raquel Quevedo is a graphic designer from Barcelona, where she was born in 1979. She graduated in Advertising and Creativity at Universitat Autónoma de Barcelona and in Art & Graphic Design at Escola Massana. So, she has a mixed education background, due to her interest to go into visual communication in depth. She is about to enter a master's course in Advanced Typography at Eina School of Art and Design in Barcelona. To complement this course of study, she has studied traditional fields of graphic design, like bookbinding and printed arts. During her studies, she worked for several worldwide agencies. After receiving the Art & Design degree, she worked for some nice, small design studios as well as undertaking work as a freelance designer in the fields of creative concepts and graphic design.

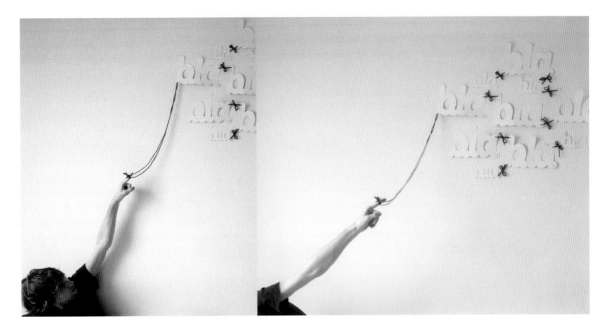

Refranes Visuales – Saying,
visual objects
(Self-initiated)
Art direction/Exhibition/Product
2009

What's your favorite part of your day?

When I have my first coffee in the morning; when my friends call me to hang out; the siesta time and also when I get sleep after a hard day of work...

What is the wildest/craziest design practice you have done over the years?

Last summer, when I was one of the winners at Incubadora/FAD awards, I had to develop a project in three months to be exhibited. It was a very tough time. I worked 8 hours for a studio and then spent the rest of my time working on the project. My life was work, work, work and more work.

Please describe a moment/thing/person that has a strong influence on your work.

I'm not a person who can be easily influenced, but I take inspiration of my surrounding, my nieces, my cat "Raimundo" and everyone who acts with no "specific" rules, without fear of being ridiculous and lately the words on street ads.

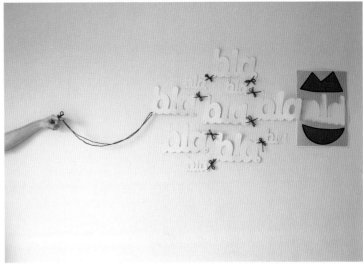

Refranes Visuales –
Saying, visual objects
(Self-initiated)
Art direction/Exhibition/
Product
2009

What has been repeatedly used in your artwork?

Strong concept, naïf style, a little bit of surrealism.

What does your work teach you?

Have fun with responsibility. Be open-minded as a child with a work purpose. Be creative without boundaries.

Who is the No.1 leading-edge designer in your mind? Ask him/her a question.

Stefan Sagmeister.
- Could I take a sabbatical year with you?

What makes you say "wooow!!" lately?

Berlin is one of the cities where I found more "wooows" - the people, the surroundings, and the special energy. In the creative field, there are some young design studios located in Barcelona as Hey Studio, Bendita Gloria, Soon in Tokyo and Diego Ramos that are developing very interesting work.

What's the most important to you now?

Be happy, enjoying my time with friends and family. Enjoy every moment of the day as a special one.

Refranes Visuales –
Saying, visual objects
(Self-initiated)
Art direction/Exhibition/
Product
2009

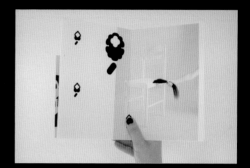

Oligo Collection
Packaging
2010

**Traslaciones del
Imaginario Report**
Graphic design
2009

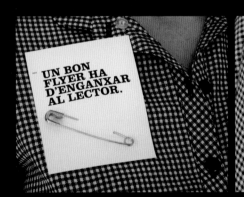

Refranes Visuales –
Saying, visual objects
(Self-initiated)
Art direction/Exhibition/
Product
2009

Sawdust are the award-winning creative partnership of Rob Gonzalez and Jonathan Quainton, an independent graphic design duo based in London. Their disciplines include art direction image-making and typography across the music, art, culture, fashion, corporate and advertising sectors.

Their approach has earned them an international reputation for creating visually striking work that is thoughtful, innovative and meticulously crafted.

Sawdust's work has been featured in internationally recognized publications, including D&AD, Lürzer's Archive, IdN, Gallery, Computer Arts, Print (New York), Novum and Los Logos: Compass.

Sawdust

Angel-A
Poster/Typographic
2010
Illustration by Sam Green

Sam Green Mailer
Printed mailer for
illustrator Sam
Green
2010
All illustrations by
Sam Green

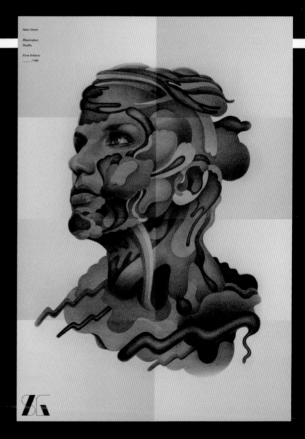

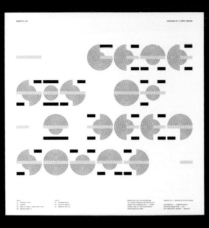

Fabrice Lig/
Fine Art Recordings
Music packaging
2010
Creative production by Edit
Photography by Andre Moore

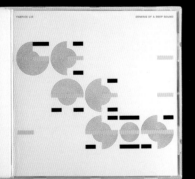

What does your typical day look like?

A typical day would go something along the lines of; arrive at 9:30(ish), have some tea, check emails, talk about who's working on what project and when things need to be delivered. Typically we'll then put some music on and then 'zone-in' to our work. If projects are in early stages and require creative direction and ideas, we'll spend our time talking it through until we come to a solution(s) that we both like, we'll then go away and explore the ideas we've come up with. At certain points we'll consult each other for direction, or to cast a fresh eye over things and then take that input on to develop it further. The hardest part in this process is not to become too precious about your work — if that happens, ideas can't be bounced and progressed to become something greater. On a good day we'll usually wrap things up for 7 - 7:30pm and head on home. On a not-so-good day, 11:30-12pm or worse...

What is the wildest/craziest design practice you have done over the years?

Not long after we set up we were contacted by an interior design company who wanted us to illustrate giant wall graphics that were to span across various rooms within a lavish penthouse apartment. It's something we had never done before — what made us nervous was the installation and getting all the measurement right because it was to be printed as large-scale vinyl stickers — so if the size was wrong there was no going back, we had to get it spot on first time. It was a daunting early job for us to undertake but it all worked out well thankfully!

Please describe a moment/thing/person that has a strong influence on your work.

We're influenced by many things and many people, recently we've been very drawn to Wim Crouwel and Total Design, but also Paul Rand, Milton Glaser, Robert Brownjohn, M.C. Escher... To name a few. We love great ideas, but crafted meticulously — two integral components — great ideas should look great.

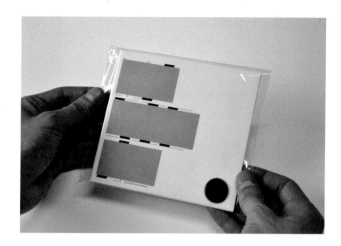

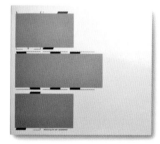

MVSICA
Music packaging
2009

What has been repeatedly used in your artwork?

We're very interested in typography and simplistic forms; it's something that features heavily in our work.

However, we would like to explore more complex and dynamic exceptions in our work as we progress, not necessarily overly simplistic or minimal.

What does your work teach you?

What we like about what we do, is that it's an ongoing study — simply put, you can never know enough. Our work teaches us that we can always improve.

Who is the No.1 leading-edge designer in your mind? Ask him/her a question.

So many people doing so many different, amazing things — there would be too many to list…

Everyone who dares to go their own way…

What makes you say "wooow!!" lately?

The Flaming Lips, I recently saw them live — and it made me go wooooow!!

What's the most important to you now?
Balance, in everything.

Computer Arts / Relentless
Editorial/Type
2010

Nude / American Classics
Editorial/Typographic illustration
2009
Illustration by Sawdust & Sneaky Raccoon

"What we like about what we do as designers is that it's an on-going study of the discipline, simply put, you can never learn enough. Our work teaches us that we can always improve."

Sérgio Alves is an emerging young designer based in the city of Porto in northern Portugal. Sérgio's designs are not limited to a specific school of idea, but rather often based on art & craft or use of organic materials within the design process. He specializes in creative and experimental design with a fresh approach to each new project, avoiding the expected and seeking always to surprise. Sérgio's inspiration can be found in other national and international designers, as well as in typical national visual stimuli such as craft, gastronomy, national culture and playful use of typography. His main focuses have been on creating posters for cultural events, editorial design and corporate identity.

USA by Designers
Poster/Illustration
2010

Bom Dia
Poster/Illustration
2009

What's your favorite part of your day?

Lunch! Lunch! Lunch! Sometimes I start thinking about lunch the night before...If I eat at home I have to start thinking about the whole creative process of making it! (I can't help myself)...I cook with whatever I find in the kitchen...This can also be a reflection of my graphic design — working

Please describe a moment/thing/person that has a strong influence on your work.

There are many small moments that together have influenced me professionally, things which led me to want to become a designer. One small major event was switching schools — I had to repeat two

What has been repeatedly used in your artwork?

What I tend to repeat is the process of trying to look at every new project in a totally different way to make it different from everything else. I adapt to the project, and not allow the project to adapt to me. I like to treat each case as completely distinct from everything else I've done — I

years of high school to change to the course I wanted...one of the best decisions I ever made! It was the new school which opened up opportunities to work with design studios on short internships and exposed me to new ideas, opportunities, and influences. Working with "Atelier Martino&Jaña" was

with what is at hand and making something new. If I wasn't a designer, I'd be a chef!

What is the wildest/craziest design practice you have done over the years?

Hummmmmm...I've been looking at this question for five minutes and can't make up my mind. I recently made a poster which would require me to kill a teddy-bear and skin him to make letters with the skin — I couldn't bring myself to harm the poor creature, what if some kids found out that I'd killed a stuffed bear? So...I found a carpet that I could use instead...and saved the bear! I like the destructive process that leads to the creative process. Creating order out of chaos.

the first time I actually saw the day-to-day of a studio, the problems, the clients; something which wouldn't have happened if I hadn't had the guts to change direction.

start from a completely blank slate with no pre-conceived ideas. It's from this process that the project seems to build itself in an organic and dynamic way. I kind of get pissed-off when I see a designer who has discovered something visually fantastic and new, and then seems to want to use nothing else except that. It gets visually tired, I think. At first it's innovative and surprising, then it's just good...after a while it's predictable, and finally becomes a cliché. That's what I want to avoid in my work.

What does your work teach you?

Never to be satisfied...always seek to improve...and be patient.

Who is the No.1 leading-edge designer in your mind? Ask him/her a question.

I couldn't possibly pick one. There are too many who are number one in their own specific way. And many leading-edge "designers" are studios with teams working on a project. So, who's the designer? The owner of the studio, or a junior partner who's working on the project?

I guess a question that I would ask any of them is: "What were you doing when you were in your early 20s?" It would be interesting to know whether they were in design early on in their lives, or if they have moved from other areas. I am sure there are hundreds of great stories.

What makes you say "wooow!!" lately?

Sushi...all you can eat for 13 euros!

What's the most important to you now?

Right now? Lunch!

...ok...I'm back from lunch now. The most important thing for me at the moment is to have my work seen. I'm working on a few projects which give me total freedom of expression — which allows me to grow as a designer. Thankfully, I don't need to worry about cash flow at the moment — I have enough for sushi.

Expoaaniferira
VI/Signage/Poster
2008
Collaboration with
Eurico Sá Fernandes

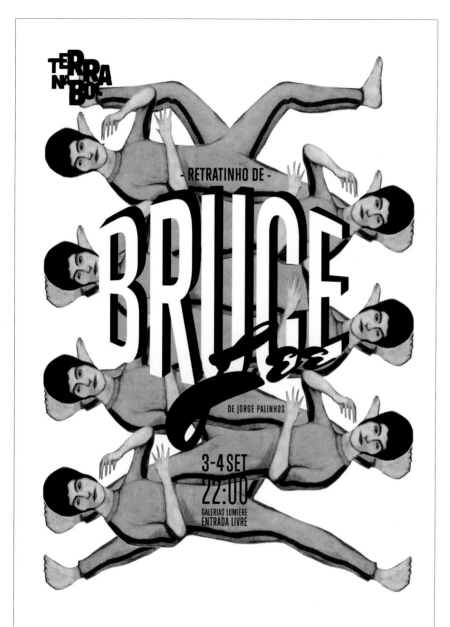

Retratinho de Bruce Lee
Poster
2010
Illustration by Alex Gozblau

"I kind of get pissed-off when I see a designer who has discovered something visually fantastic and new, and then seems to want to use nothing else except that. It gets visually tired, I think. At first it's innovative and surprising, then it's just good... after a while it's predictable, and finally becomes a cliché. That's what I want to avoid in my work."

Shogo Kishino

Born in 1975 in Tokyo. In 1996, Shogo Kishino graduated from Tokyo YMCA Institute of Design. Worked at Hiromura Design Office from 1996 to 2007, and then established 6D.

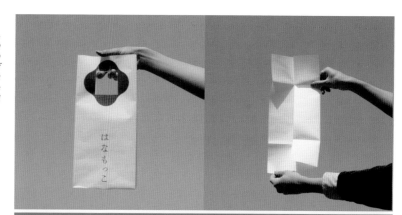

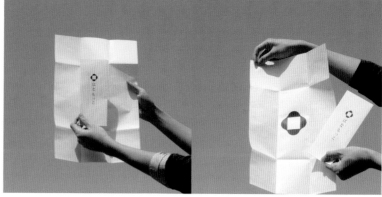

Hanamokko
Packaging design
2009

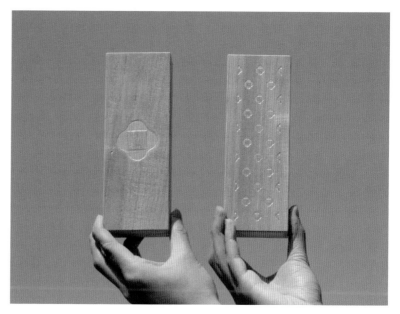

What do you look like?

Someone says I look horrible. (Laugh)

What does your typical day look like?

I work over 14 hours a day, 6 days a week. It started when I was still an assistant. Now it has been 14 years – though I work a long time, it is nothing special when I keep doing it everyday. As the saying goes, no pain, no gain. I believe that as long as I work hard, the reward will come one day.

What is the wildest/craziest design practice you have done over the years?

Those experimental art works I made for exhibition, but not those I made in usual days. I will always try to use something new in my graphic design.

Please describe a moment/thing/person that has a strong influence on your work.

When I was longing to become a designer, ADC Annual gives the most important influence on me. It was around 1995 that graphic design was prevalent in advertising in Japan.

What has been repeatedly used in your artwork?

I try not to repeat the same graphic elements in my work, but I will apply the same process to work out a project. My reasoning and logic will help to make my work done.

What is the most important thing you learned when designing?

I have a teacher. I can still remember how he worked and that was impressive. I learned a lot from him.

MINATO
DOG

Minatodog
VI
2008

**Who is the No.1 designer in your mind?
Ask him/her a question.**

I admire all the designers except myself. I would like to know, "Do you feel guilty when you are having a break?"

What makes you say "wooow!!" lately?

Lately, I received The JAGDA New Designer Award 2010. A dream of 14 years finally comes true. I wasn't "wooow" that moment; I was almost excited to faint out.

What's the most important to you now?

Work. The most important thing is to balance my commissioned projects and the self-initiated ones.

"*I work over 14 hours a day, 6 days a week. It starts when I was still an assistant. Now it has been 14 years – though I work a long time, it is nothing special when I keep doing it everyday. As the saying goes, no pain, no gain. I believe that as long as I work hard, the reward will come one day.*"

Yokohama Sky Building Entrance
Signage
2008

Vending Machine
Product design
2009

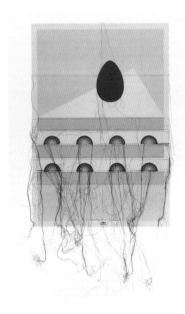
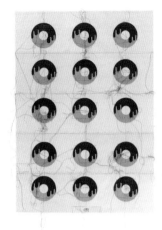
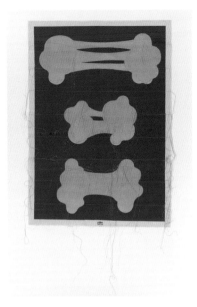

JAGDA TOKYO JUNK
Poster
2009

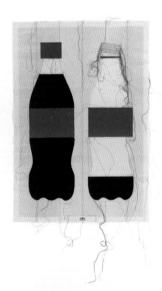
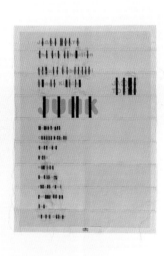

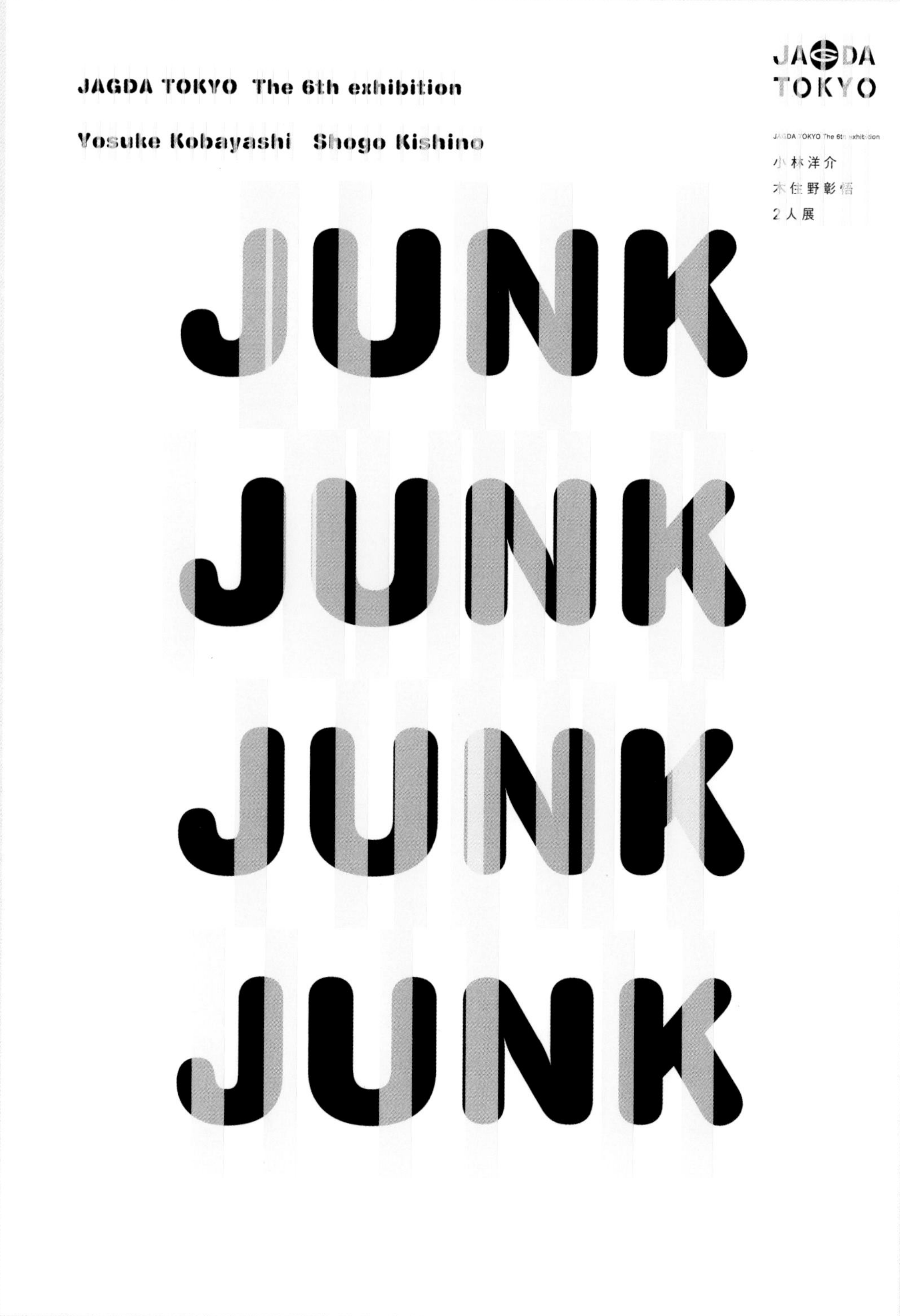
JAGDA TOKYO The 6th exhibition
Yosuke Kobayashi Shogo Kishino
JAGDA TOKYO
JAGDA TOKYO The 6th exhibition
小林洋介
木住野彰悟
2人展
JUNK
JUNK
JUNK
JUNK

6D
VI
2008

Onda Design
VI
2008

Sato Takuma Design Office
VI
2008

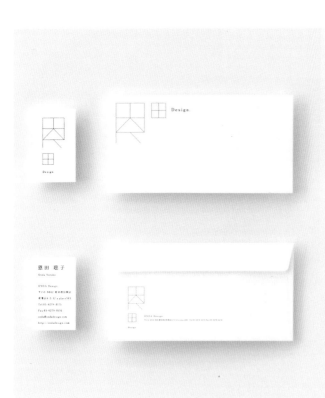

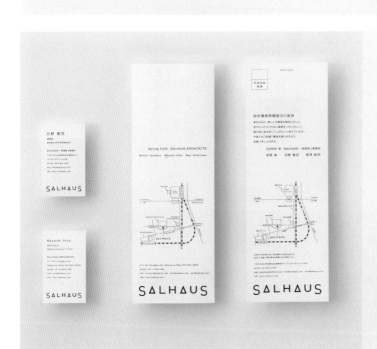

So Hashizume

Monkicho
Book design
2009

So, what does your typical day look like?
Walking, talking, eating, cycling...
Everything is connected to what I do now. I love everyday ordinariness here.

What is the wildest/craziest design practice you have done over the years?
I had a 3-day bookshop in a hotel room in Kyoto. I gathered lots of independent magazines, smallzines etc. Many of them were on a bed, some on a table and few on a glass...

What has been repeatedly used in your artwork?
Theory, rule, rumor, system, order.
Pen, conversation, walking, library... sometimes nap.

What distinguishes your work from that of your contemporaries?
I don't really like to make things complex...

Who is the No.1 leading-edge designer in your mind? Ask him/her a question.
Hello, you must enjoy your life.

What is the best part of being a designer?
Let people smile:)

What would you like to be if you were not a designer?
Make a cup of coffee listening 60's music in the room with some of my favourite books. Friends welcome.

What makes you say "wooow!!" lately?
Two spiders fighting on the wall of my studio!

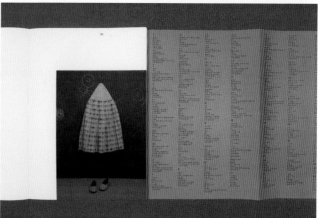

So Hashizume is a graphic designer currently working in Tokyo, Japan. He graduated from the Communication Art & Design Department at the Royal College of Art in London in 2006. His works focus on exploration of new possibility for communication design in the fields of graphic design, editorial design, web design and workshops.

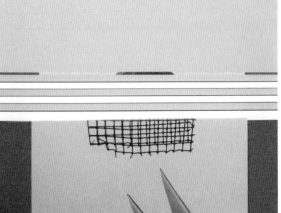

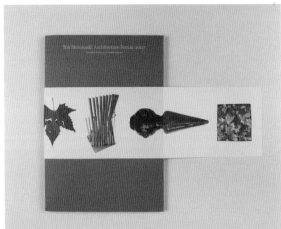

"I don't really like to make things complex..."

Toh Shimazaki Architecture Forum
Book design
2007

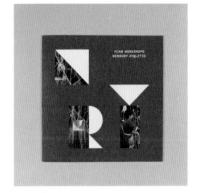

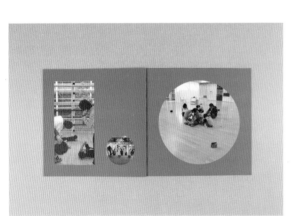

YCAM Workshops
Book design
2009

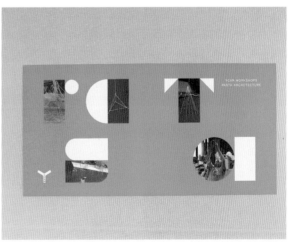

Sublima
Comunicación

"To appreciate the quality of things and not to be content with the first thing I see. Be more demanding with everything around me."

Sublima was founded in 2002 in the city of Murcia (Spain) as a creative communication agency, but it rather calls itself "a company of ideas". All developments in the world, everything around us comes from an idea, a thought. That is the basis of Sublima – the search for concepts applies to a design which transmits many things just using a few. A search that applies to editorial design, corporate identity, packaging, advertising, direct marketing, street marketing... and everything that requires implementing a creative idea to solve a problem, generally, of communication.

How did you get the name "Sublima"?

It came from the word "Sublimation" which is the transition of a substance from the solid phase to the gas phase without passing through an intermediate liquid phase
It came up to our mind because of the transition the ideas make: from the mind directly to the paper.

What is the wildest/craziest design practice you have done over the years?

We designed and organized an outdoor festival in the center of Murcia. One of the activities was to prepare a huge cake typical for Christmas in Spain called "Roscón" for 100 people.

Please describe a moment/thing/person that has a strong influence on your work.

There are many designers who have influenced my work. Designers and friends here in the city of Murcia that have been a reference, as well as other internationals. But it was my borther who greatly influenced the way I work, the passion and energy he gave to his job. How positive and enthusiastic he was at work. That energy has been what most influenced me.

What has been repeatedly used in your artwork?

There was a specific time that we used to use vectorial ornaments and illustrations. We are very careful with typography and concepts, but each project and each client is different so we try not to repeat and give each one a work as "unique" as possible.

What does your work teach you?

To appreciate the quality of things and not to be content with the first thing I see. Be more demanding with everything around me.

Who is the No.1 leading-edge designer in your mind? Ask him/her a question.

It's difficult to say! There are many amazing designers. I woldn't say just one but if I get focus in Spain I would say MARISCAL. I've always liked his work because of the ability he has to design for any sector and the illusion that it has after many years working. I would ask: How can you keep that energy and passion after so many years working?

Club de autor
Poster
2009

What makes you say "wooow!!" lately?

A thousand things! Almost everything that strikes me makes me say "guauuuu." Could be a good work, a good concert, good food, or someone who surprised me...

What's the most important to you now?

My family is always the most important thing for me, and the people I have close relationship with - friends and colleagues.

But from the professional point of view the most important thing for me is that we stay together for many years doing what we really like and doing it with the freedom we have.

Ok Textil
VI
2009

enero	febrero	marzo	abril
mayo	junio	julio	agosto
septiembre	octubre	noviembre	diciembre

2009
www.oktextil.com

CEINCIANÍA
Logo
2010

 ciencianía

 zikitrake

 best wishes

 ciencia divertida

No le gusta la comida. ▲

No quiere que quede con nadie. ▲

Se ha tomado cuatro cervezas. ▲

▲ Me ha visto saludando a un vecino.

Me ha dicho que a la próxima me mata. ▲

TÚ PUEDES BORRARLO DEL MAPA.
Campaña contra la violencia de género.

Consejería de Política Social, Mujer e Inmigración

✱ ¿Cómo dices NO a la violencia de género? • Opina en **www.facebook.com/imujer**

Región de Murcia   Instituto de la Mujer de la Región de Murcia

Calendar 2010
Self-promotion
2010

CENDEAC
Print
2009

Este curso pretende proporcionar, tanto a un público no iniciado como a los aficionados no especialistas, recursos suficientes para acercarse con espíritu crítico al arte contemporáneo y al contexto cultural en el que surge. A partir del comentario de las imágenes más significativas del arte de los últimos 50 años discutirá las razones por las que han adquirido esa consideración de privilegio en su contexto sociocultural, sin simplificarlas pero sin complicarlas.

Programa
Este curso constará de seis temas
impartidos en cinco sesiones

Información adicional

1.
La epopeya de la nostalgia, o ¿Por qué los artistas ya no saben dibujar?

3.
El espíritu contracultural de la vanguardia, o ¿Por qué los artistas ya no hacen obras de arte?

5.
El postmodernismo apocalíptico, o ¿Por qué los artistas son tan protestones?

2.
Autonomía y alienación, o ¿Por qué los artistas trabajan ahora tan poco?

4.
El postmodernismo integrado, o ¿Por qué a los artistas les interesa la banal?

6.
Figuras dúctiles en un fondo siniestro, o ¿Por qué los artistas se han vuelto tan cursilas?

"Todo lo que usted siempre quiso saber sobre arte y nadie le explicó" o Las contradicciones culturales del arte del capitalismo.

Curso de introducción al arte contemporáneo, impartido por Ramón Salas.

Del 12 al 16 de abril.
18.00 h.

Surya Prasetya, a Melbourne based graphic designer, works on a range of projects in the areas of Art Direction, Typography, Publication, Brand Development and Printed Material. His style of design is clean, simple and different.

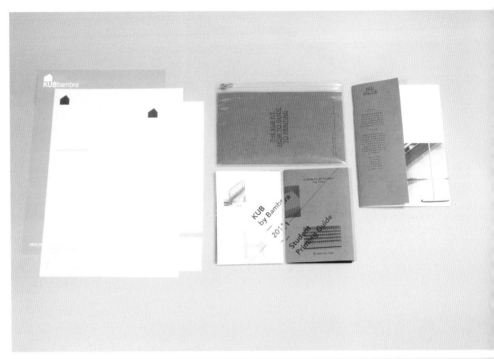

Surya
Prasetya

What does your typical day look like?

Wake up, get a coffee. Start up my computer.

What is the wildest/craziest design practice you have done over the years?

Wild and crazy doesn't really fit in with my style of work.

Please describe a moment/stuff/person that gives you a strong influence on your profession.

I think all the people around me, they put me in my place to make sure I stay focused. Being aware of current design trends constantly so that you can keep pushing yourself, this is what makes it interesting.

What has been repeatedly used in your artwork?

I think photography & basic elements that will always compliment the simplicity that I try to stay loyal to.

What does your work teach you?

It teaches you discipline, to always better/challenge yourself.

Who is the No.1 leading-edge designer in your mind? Ask him/her a question.

I don't know about individuals but I have always been a big fan of "Experimental Jetset." I have always been attracted to their simplicity.

What makes you say "wooow!!" lately?

Watching "Grand Designs".

What's the most important to you now?

Slowly growing/enjoying the progression.

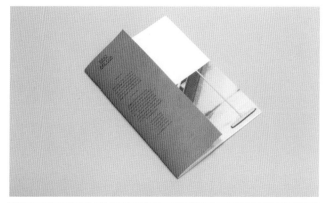

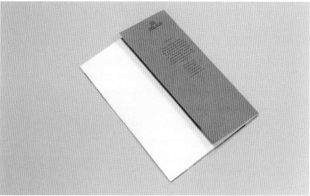

KUB
Identity and mailer kit
2010

Concrete Soul
Publication
2010

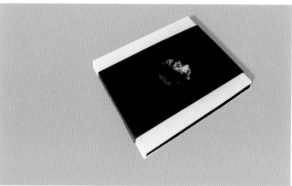

"Slowly growing/enjoying the progression."

Yoshimi
Typography/Packaging
2010

Swollen is an award winning Dublin based graphic design studio founded in 2006 by Rory McCormick and Rossi McAuley.

Christy Moore –
Live at Barrowland
DVD
2009

Rory, what's your favorite part of your day?

Can't really say, sending something to print is good and then receiving stuff from printers is good too. Also getting paid, breakfast, nice coffee, a beer on any given day etc.

What is the wildest/craziest design practice you have done over the years?

While working on a project for Amnesty International we designed, assembled and painted 32 4ft x 4ft cubes. The craziest part was that we undertook the painting of the cubes ourselves. Each cube had five sides with one side left open. Each side in turn required 3-4 coats of paint. So this means in order to complete the cubes we painted an area of 10,240 square feet in 5 days.

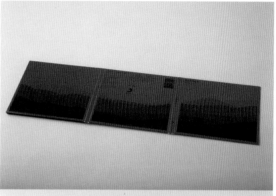

Please describe a moment/thing/person that has a strong influence on your work.

Rory: David Smith (recently elected to the AGI), my tutor from college.

Rossi: Anything where form and fuction combine to make something unique.

Rossi, if Rory were a sound, what would it be?

Very distinctive.

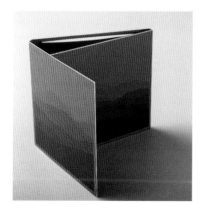

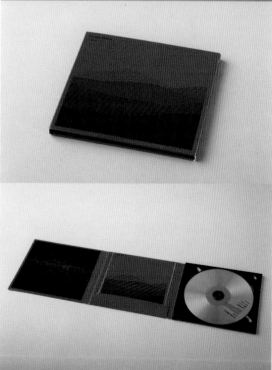

Rory, if Rossi were a smell, what would it be?

A musty cosmopolitan.

What has been repeatedly used in your artwork?

Rory: A stong grid.

Rossi: Close attention to detail in printing.

Who is the No.1 leading-edge designer in your mind? Ask him/her a question.

Rory: Money's Too Tight to Mention. What makes you say wow lately?

Rossi: I don't really believe that there is any one leading-edge designer so I couldn't name a specific person, I don't really think about design as something where any one person can be the best. However there are plenty of studios or individual designers I admire.

What makes you say "wooow!!" lately?

Rory: Nice homes and designs where I can't see a grid.

Rossi: Bridges.

What's the most important to you now?
Rory: Good clients and then some.
Rossi: Maintaining consistency.

Amnesty International Ireland –
Hear My Voice
Packaging
2010
Photography: Seanandyvette

Royal Institute of Architects (RIAI) – Open House
Poster
2009

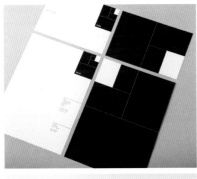

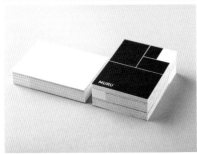

Muru
Corporate identity
2009

Carolina Hoffman and the Lighthouse cinema –
Bouvard et Pecuchet
Poster
2009

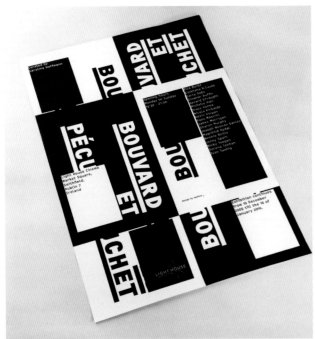

"Maintaining consistency."

le cool
Poster
2010

Tilman Schlevogt (born 1983) is a designer living and working in Stuttgart and Berlin, Germany. He is co-founder of the independent publishing house "Edition Taube" and is part of "the forever ending story", an international curatorial project. Tilman Schlevogt has won several design awards including TDC New York, TDC Tokyo, Red Dot, and Most Beautiful Books of Germany.

"Designing should be fun. Sometimes I forget that. I shouldn't take it too serious."

Tilman
Schlevogt

THE CONSTANT SEARCH

What's your favorite part of your day?

I prefer working at night.
But I love the silent early morning, when I'm
still awake.

**What is the wildest/craziest design practice
you have done over the years?**

I'm boring.

**Please describe a moment/thing/person
that has a strong influence on your work.**

The best ideas come to my mind when I'm
out cycling.

**What has been repeatedly used in your
artwork?**

Many many doubts.

What does your work teach you?

Designing should be fun. Sometimes I forget
that. I shouldn't take it too serious, cause
there's always someone better.

**Who is the No.1 leading-edge designer in
your mind? Ask him/her a question.**

I don't do rankings in principle.

What makes you say "wooow!!" lately?

Seeing my girlfriend.

What's the most important to you now?

Friends and Music.

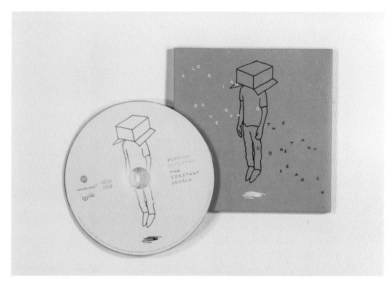

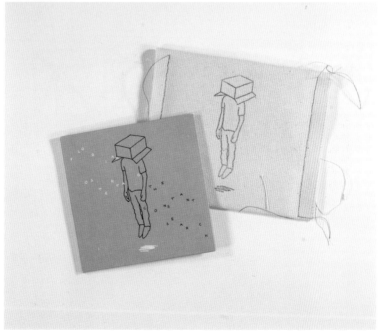

Künstlerhaus Stuttgart
CI/Posters/Flyers/Exhibition design
2009-2011
Collaboration with Jonas Beuchert

**The Academy, The Art,
The Professors**
Book
2010
Collaboration with Jonas
Beuchert

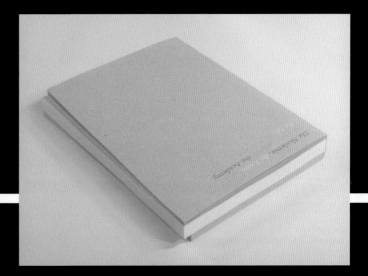

What We Know
Book
2009
Collaboration with Jonas
Beuchert and Patrick Oltean

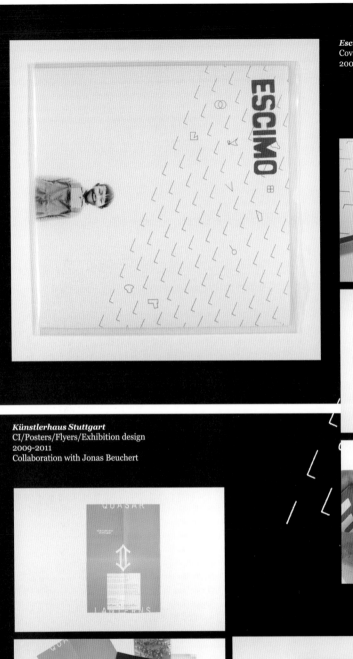

Escimo
Cover artwork
2006

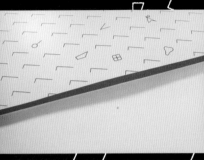

Künstlerhaus Stuttgart
CI/Posters/Flyers/Exhibition design
2009-2011
Collaboration with Jonas Beuchert

Tore
Cheung

Tore Cheung creates drawing, paintings and collages. He is a Hong Kong based designer who happens to make art. To be more precise, he is a visual artist who occasionally designs. He received his BA in visual communication from Polytechnic University of Hong Kong. Upon graduation, he has been freelancing with his beginner's luck. He has managed to cross disciplines with his art in the fields of editorial, fashion, music and more.

"I should have done it better."

***Milk Design Photo Frame
Insert Artwork***
Illustration
2007

Initial Fashion FW o8'
"Comprehension"
Fashion illustration
2008

*Daydream
Nation AW 2010
Collaboration T-shirt*
Fashion illustration
2008

*Daydream Nation
"Random" T-shirt*
Fashion illustration
2010

Self-promotion Poster Booklet
Print
2007

What's your favorite part of your day?
Morning.
Everything seems hopeful before lunch.

What is the wildest/craziest design practice you have done over the years?
I wanted to design a CD sleeve so badly that I started a band.

Please describe a moment/thing/person that has a strong influence on your work.
Accidents. Accidents allow me to go beyond my expected outcome.

What has been repeatedly used in your artwork?
Skull, blood and heart-shaped sunglasses.

What does your work teach you?
I should have done it better.

Who is the No.1 leading-edge designer in your mind? Ask him/her a question.
Gary Cards.

What makes you say "wooow!!" lately?
A slide-viewing TV toy designed by chi hoi, a Hong Kong based artist.

What's the most important to you now?
My health.

Trapped in Suburbia

Trapped in Suburbia is a smart creative studio based in the Hague, the Netherlands. They enjoy working at the cutting edge, challenging themselves and those around them, looking further than the length of their nose. They create conceptually and strategically strong projects with clear, clever designs and solutions. They think before they act, but they act before they talk. They love telling stories and inspiring people, doing extensive research and pushing boundaries. To drink from a cup that's half empty and have fun. Next to the design agency they also run the contemporary graphic art gallery Ship of Fools.

How did you get the name "Trapped in Suburbia"?

Trapped in Suburbia was born in the beginning of 2004 in Mariahoeve, a suburb of The Hague, Holland. It all started with Cuby Gerards and Karin Langeveld working from their home, a tiny apartment on the third floor. And because we like to use humor in our work we thought it was a good idea put a little humor in the name as well. Hence the name "Trapped in Suburbia".

What is the wildest/craziest design practice you have done over the years?

That would be the new exhibition design for a basement filled with medieval torture

equipment. We started to think how to make it more exciting and get kids to read the little signs next to the torture equipment. We've decided to make it an experience

by putting all the information on the floor with UV-paint. In this way you can only see something when you put on the UV-flash light otherwise it is just a white floor. So you have to wander around with a torch and really have to go exploring and discover new things. All the info on the floor is hand drawn, even the text.

Please describe a moment/thing/person that has a strong influence on your work.

We love Pictoplasma! It's not a graphic design conference but more about illustration, character design and urban art. We like the way these people approach creativity. We find it very inspiring and it makes us happy!

What has been repeatedly used in your artwork?

We always try to put a little or a lot of humor in our designs, that makes us happy and the people who see it.

What does your work teach you?

It teaches us to be inventive and use techniques in new ways.

Who is the No.1 leading-edge designer in your mind? Ask him/her a question.

For us there isn't really a number one, everyone has their own quality but we like

the works of: Stefan Sagmeister, Milkxhake, Kessels Kramer, Alex Trochut, Noma Bar, and of course the incredible guys of Jonge Meesters.

The question would be: "Hi guys, how are you doing? Would you be interested in a big collaboration project?"

What makes you say "wooow!!" lately?

We actually organize a typographic festival called "Don't believe the type" and because of this we see a lot of nice powerful typography. We love the work of Sean Freeman and Jeff Canham!

What's the most important to you now?

The collaboration between us, we (Cuby & Karin) started Trapped in Suburbia together and we are creative partners and life partners. This brings certain chemistry to the design, which is really important.

Campaign Love Life Festival
Branding
2009

Design It Yourself
Exhibition design for
Graphic Design Museum
2011

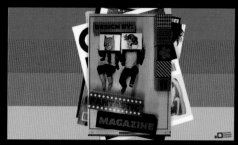

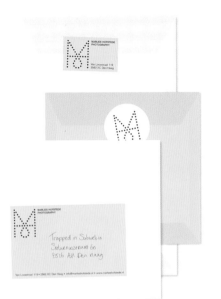

Marlies Hofstede
Identity
2010

Gouda bij Kunstlicht
Identity
2008

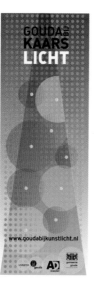

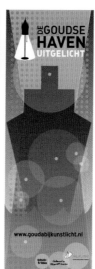

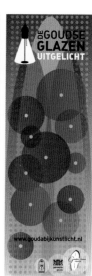

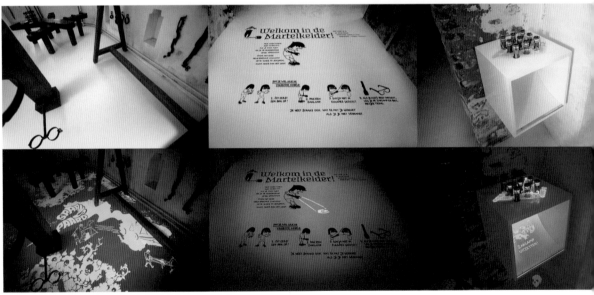

Torture Basement
Exhibition design
2010

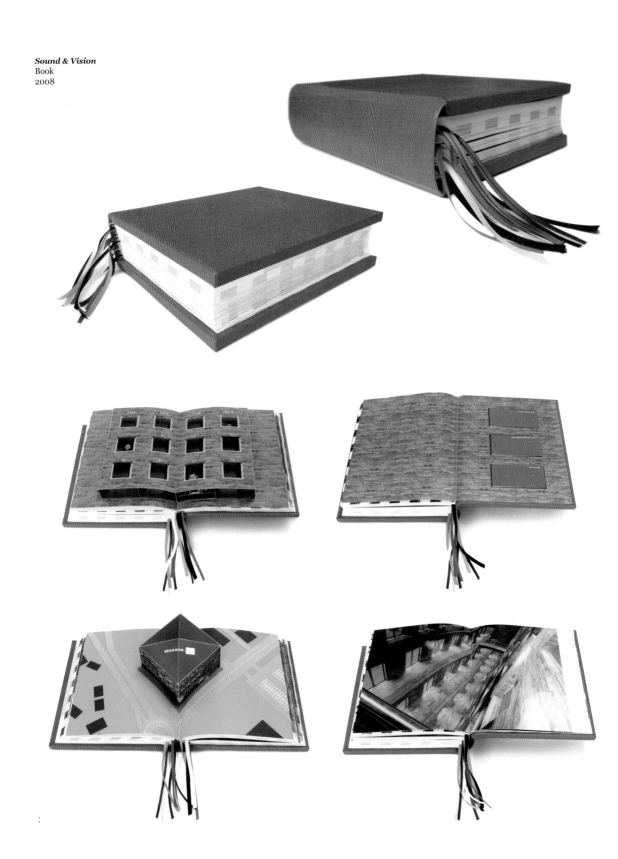

VJ Movement
Book
2009

»THE REALITY IS PEOPLE ARE GOING TO DECIDE TO COME HERE BECAUSE THEY'RE RUNNING FOR THEIR LIVES

PEOPLE ON THE MOVE

»THIS IS A HUGE GLOBAL CRISIS, JUST UNDER A BILLION PEOPLE LACK ACCESS TO WATER.«

NATURAL RESOURCES

THERE IS ONE TRUTH

THERE IS MORE THAN ONE TRUTH

"We always try to put a little or a lot of humor in our designs, that makes us happy and the people who see it."

Two Dot Two is a multi-disciplinary communication studio, established in Porto (Portugal) by Maria Helena Silva and João Bento Soares.

2 brains with 4 arms and 4 hands: the main tools for creation. Their work is often described as tactile and fresh, with traces of human emotions, in a lucid and fun way. From concept to final artwork, most of all, they enjoy the process. Every project is a unique way to express ideas, using exhaustive research and analysis, out-of-the-box thinking and curiosity. They like to blur the boundaries between work areas, developing concepts for various media, printed and digital.

Feiras Francas
Exhibition
2010

<u>João, how did you get the name To Dot Two?</u>

When we started working 🖤 👥 together in 2007 we didn't have a name.
As the work came along we realized that we were completing each other. So the name came to us in a very simple way.
We work as a duo, using two Brains two hands each.

<u>João, could you give me some words about Maria?</u>

She is exotic, Intelligent, she is the kind of person that

Inspires me.

When she is not ILLustrating long haired girls with cats Body or designing a band album cover,

She is reading.

At work I dream a Lot sometimes, I go out of the guide Limes (dreaming is not bad but when im the correct place) and she gets me in place.

When we are working on something new, we look at eachother and see in the same way.

MY hand is her arm HER HEART IS MY MONSTER

A leading-edge designer in your mind? Ask him/her a question.

Can I take your Picture? Do you swim?
Do you own a cat or a dog? what kind of underware
do you use? How Do you feel when you finish an artwork?

What would you like to be if you were not a designer?

A Chef, I love to cook as much as I love to paint

João, what makes you say "wooow!!" recently?

each time I go pick UP my Developed Film
and I see the pictures, each time I stumble
upon a new creation.

Time
Illustration
2009
Illustration by Maria Helena

Maria, could you give me some words about João?

João is an artist, multimedia designer & illustrator. He's super creative, always looking for new ways to work & communicate. You can easily find him drawing, seating in the subway or looking though the viewfinder of his camera, or sneaking behind you to capture you on film. He he also crazy, making crazy drawings & crazy movies.

Maria, what is the wildest/craziest design practice you have done over the years?

We spent literally an entire summer, drawing & writting postcards for 600 PEOPLE. We had the idea of personally invite the residents of VILA NOVA DE CERVEIRA, to come and visit the International ART Fair, that's in town during August / september. We noticed that most of these people did'nt even know what the FAIR was about. We wanted to start a new level of proximity between the ART Fair and the local people. Also, we wanted to Bring back the magic of receiving a handwriten postcard. So, we invited everyone to come to the Fair & Bring along their invitation postcard. The postcards were placed on a wall, and .... like a puzzel, an intire image would show up. Needless to say it was a lot of Fun but our hands had bruises from all the drawing, writing and puzzel making.

What has been repeatedly used in your artwork?

Some of our work is totally digital BUT mostly we like to use our HANDS. Most of our work has some kind of hand drawing or handwriting tipography. We LIKE to use human touch & EMOTIONS. Perhaps, we are a Bit of an Old Fashion kind of studio, with our stop-motion animations, pensils, stains, ink, photografs & stationary.

<u>A leading-edge designer in your mind? Ask him/her a question.</u>

Dear Everyone who inspires me everyday, what is your darkest secret?

<u>Maria, what is the best part of being a designer?</u>

→ working on different projects every week or month;

→ Learning about lot's of new stuff in the way;

→ Satisfaction of a Happy client;

→ Possibly making people's life better or happier;

→ Surprising people;

→ turning consepts into objects;

→ Mastering the art of making hand drawings of arrows, not quite there yet.

<u>What would you like to be if you were not a designer?</u>

A WRITER.
I like to tell stories.

Postcards Invitations
Promotion for XV
International Art Biennale
in Vila Nova de Cerveira
2009

2010 Calendar
Illustration
2009
Illustration By Maria Helena

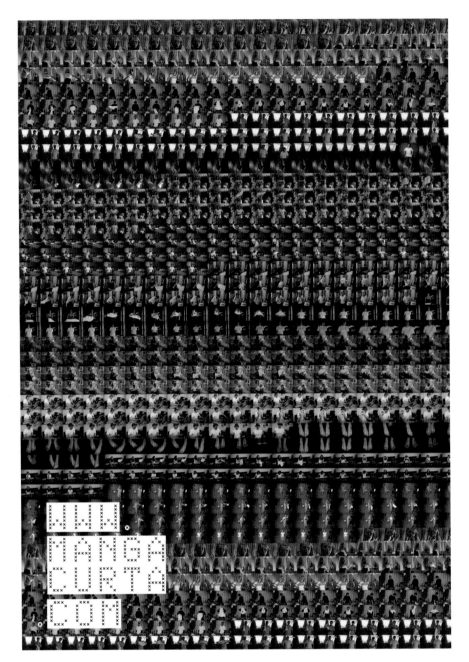

"*Working on different projects every week or month; learning about lots of new stuff along the way; the satisfaction of a happy client; possibly making people's life better or happier; surprising people; turning concepts into objects; mastering the act of making hand drawings of arrows, not quite there yet.*"

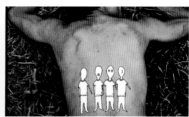

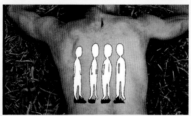
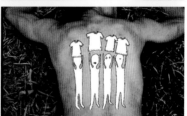

***Paredes de Coura's
Music Festival***
Stop-motion video
2008

Fill in the Blank
Stop-motion video/Graphic
design
2007

What does your typical day look like?

Something like this: coffee, work, coffee, work, coffee, work, coffee, work, eat, coffee, work, coffee, work, coffee, work, beer, work, beer, work, beer.

What is the wildest/craziest design practice you have done over the years?

Recently we tried to print a flyer with lemon juice, to get secret writing which can be made visible by heating it up with a lighter. We're still on it to perfect the process. It's quite tricky to get the right consistency of the lemon juice. And we tried to glue popcorn together to get a hand made font.

Please describe a moment/thing/person that has a strong influence on your work.

Lately we discover more and more the reduced way and beauty of typography. We really started to like the Swiss graphic design of the 50', 60'. To use typography not only as informal text, but to create an image, a visual story with letters and the way they are used.

We really like the work of Hans-Rudolf Lutz. He has a very strong influence on our work.

What has been repeatedly used in your artwork?

We always try to involve handwork to the design process, to experiment with different printing techniques and materials. And we like to use: strong typography, black and white and informal graphics.

Type Fabric is a small graphic design studio in Switzerland consisting of Samuel Egloff and Catrina Wipf. After studying graphic design together the studio was founded right away in August 2009.

What does your work teach you?
Life.

Who is the No.1 leading-edge designer in your mind? Ask him/her a question.
We don't think that there is one No.1 designer. There are so many good designers out there and each one of them has their own way of working, so many styles, people, personalities. There is no way of comparing. Just enjoying and sharing.

What makes you say "wooow!!" lately?
"wow" with one "o"s would be our first self brewed beer called: A-Bier.
"woow" with two "o"s: the swiss tv show "Landfrauenküche".
And "wooow" with three "o"s must be the word itself.

What's the most important to you now?
Samuel: My Swiss army knife.

Catrina: B-Bier.

La Fête
Invitation/T-shirts
2010

Type Fabric Shirts

Type Fabric Shirts

Mnevis
Artwork
2010

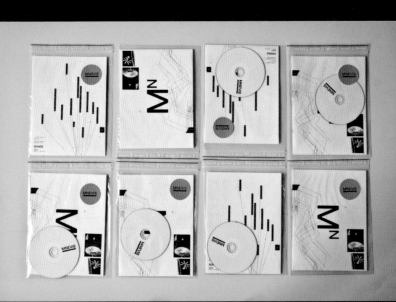

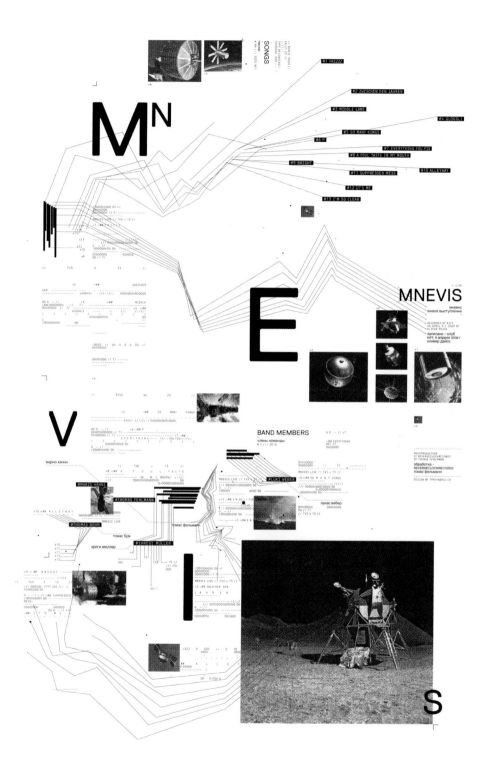

MᴺEVIS

SONGS

#1 FRIZZZ
#2 ZWISCHEN DEN JAHREN
#3 MIDDLE LANE
#4 GLOGGLI
#5 SO MANY KINGS
#6 P
#7 EVERYTHING YOU FIX
#8 A FOUL TASTE IN MY MOUTH
#9 BRIGHT
#10 ALLEYWAY
#11 SUPPRESSED MESS
#12 IT'S ME
#13 I'M SO CLEAR

MNEVIS

LIVE

МНЕВИС
живов выступление

RECORDED AT KIFF
ON APRIL 9 / 2009 BY
OLIVER DEISS

записано – клуб
KIFF, 9 апреля 2009 г
оливер дайсс

BAND MEMBERS

члены команды

#MARIO HÄNNI — марио хэнни
#THOMAS FEHLMANN — томас фельманн
#THOMAS BOHM — томас бум
#CHREGT MULLER — хриги мюллер
#LUKI WEBER — лукас вебер

POSTPRODUCTION
AT REVERSECLOCKRECORDS
BY THOMAS FEHLMANN

обработка –
REVERSECLOCKRECORDS
ТОМАС ФЕЛЬМАНН

DESIGN BY TYPEFABRIC.CH

Located in Seoul, Korea, workroom is a graphic design studio and publishing house. In December 2006, four people - a photographer, an editor and two graphic designers - jointly opened the studio. Since then, workroom has primarily worked on community design and publishing as well as design services for clients. In addition, workroom helps run Gagarin, a second-hand bookstore opened in 2008 that specializes in art and design.

Aland
Brand identity
2010

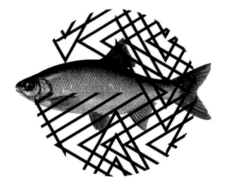

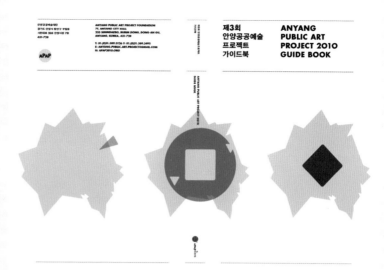

ANYANG PUBLIC ART PROJECT FOUNDATION
7F, ANYANG CITY HALL
235 SIMINDAERO, DONGAN GU,
ANYANG, KOREA, 431-728

제3회
안양공공예술
프로젝트
가이드북

ANYANG
PUBLIC ART
PROJECT 2010
GUIDE BOOK

What does a leading-edge designer look like?

If there was a look that a leading-edge designer had, I would want to have that look – as long as it didn't involve plastic surgery.

How did you get the name Workroom?

It's been more than three years since we launched this studio. Time really flies. At first, we thought hard about our name, but to be honest I've forgotten why we spent so much time thinking about it or how we even come up with the name Workroom. All of just wanted a name that was kind of neutral and that would not make us sick and tired of it many years down the road. Three years on, everyone here still likes the name Workroom.

What is the wildest/craziest design practice you have done over the years?

There's a type of paper we've used quite a lot since the end of last year. It's a thin piece of paper that's used for making cheap envelopes, though it is rarely used for books because it results in a poor quality of printing. Actually, it's almost impossible to use for offset printing because of static electricity in winter. In any event, we keep using it. It's pretty crazy because every piece of paper should be arranged by hand after printing on one side in order to print on the other side. However, we continue to use this paper despite these challenges, so I think the head of the printing house is ready to kill us.

What has been repeatedly used in your artwork?

As I said, there are things that we prefer in terms of paper, typefaces, and graphic elements during certain periods, but such preferences are pursued on a continual basis. For example, one spring we'll use

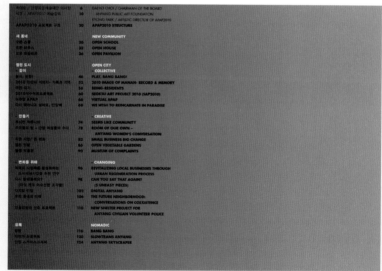

Universe 55 and that summer we'll switch to Akzidenz Grotesk bold. I think what we think highly of and what everyone here at the studio shares in common is the sense of rhythm caused by the management of typography.

What distinguishes your work from that of your contemporaries?

These days, there are so many talented designers out there. Everybody is doing amazing works. I think the difference lies not in their design ability but in who they

work with. Workroom mainly has clients from the field of art and culture, especially individual artists and smaller clients. This allows us to maintain our identity in a relatively free atmosphere.

A leading-edge designer in your mind? Ask him/her a question.

What do you think you will be doing 10 years from now? Oh, and do you smoke?

Artist of the Year
2009 – Suh Yong-sun
Exhibition/Invitation
2009

mk2
Postcard
2008/2010

올해의
작가
2009
서용선

초대일시
2009. 7. 2. 목. 오후 5시

전시기간
2009. 7. 3. 금. –
2009. 9. 20. 일.

장소
국립현대미술관
제1전시실 및 중앙홀

국립현대미술관은 한국의 현대미술을
한 차원 높은 수준으로 끌어올리는
작가의 대형 개인전으로
올해의 작가 2009 – 서용선展을 개최합니다.
부디 개막식에 참석하셔서
자리를 빛내주시기 바랍니다.

2009년 6월
국립현대미술관장 배순훈

Artist of
the Year
2009
Suh Yong-sun

opening reception
July 2, 2009 17:00

exhibition period
July 3, 2009 –
September 20, 2009

exhibition venue
Gallery 1 and Main Hall of
National Museum of
Contemporary Art, Korea

National Museum of
Contemporary Art, Korea
requests the pleasure of
your company at the exhibition,
Artist of the Year 2009 -
Suh Yong-sun

June 2009.
Soonhoon Bae
Director of
National Museum of
Contemporary Art, Korea

mk2

opening hour /
11:00-23:00

address /
122-2
changseong-dong
jongro-gu,
seoul, korea

telephone /
82-2-730-6420
email /
designmk2@gmail.com

mk2

opening hour /
11:00-23:00

address /
122-2
changseong-dong
jongro-gu,
seoul, korea

telephone /
82-2-730-6420
email /
designmk2@gmail.com

mk2

opening hour /
11:00-23:00

address /
122-2
changseong-dong
jongro-gu,
seoul, korea

telephone /
82-2-730-6420
email /
designmk2@gmail.com

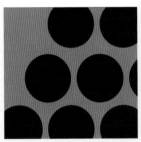

What is the best part of being a designer?

Designers are constantly working on something, but they don't actually make anything all by themselves. We just put together proposals and commission the production of things. Still, we enjoy the pleasure of creating something by hand. What we feel the moment we receive freshly printed materials is the greatest reward that a graphic designer can have. The problem is that there's never anything more than that.

What would you like to be if you were not a designer?

I would be someone who gets to look over incredible printed materials. I'd be an editor.

What makes you say "wooow!!" lately?

Getting invited to designer Sulki Choi's exhibition, where the place itself was expressed as overlapped diagrams. The invitation was interesting. The envelope was delivered to us, but without anything inside. It just had the date and venue for the exhibition printed on the outside of the envelope. I told my friend sitting next to me, "There's nothing else in it". He replied, "Really"? Then at the bottom of the envelope I found the name of the exhibition which reads "really?". Graphic designer Julia Born's exhibition, which was held in Leipzig last fall, was also very impressive. The exhibition itself became a book and the book became a space again – it was great.

printing
binding
special effect

hyosung printing

219
inhyundong-2ga, jung-gu,
seoul, korea

t. 82-2-2261-0006
f. 82-2-2269-8436

i was
in a printing-house
in hell, and saw
the method
in which
knowledge
is transmitted
from
generation

▼

to
generation

william blake

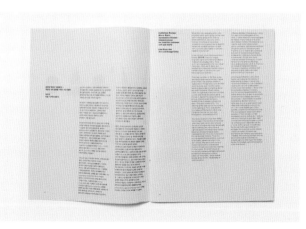

Hyosung Printing
Ads
2010

Kim Min-ae
Book Design
2009

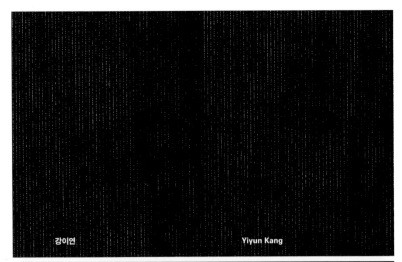

The Trickster
Book
2010
Featured artwork goes
to artist Yiyun Kang.

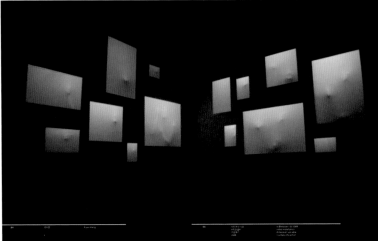

"*Designers are constantly working on something, but they don't actually make anything all by themselves. We just put together proposals and commission the production of things. Still, we enjoy the pleasure of creating something by hand. What we feel the moment we receive freshly printed materials is the greatest reward that a graphic designer can have. The problem is that there's never anything more than that.*"

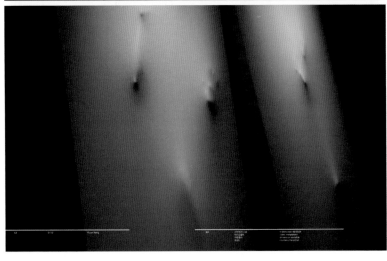

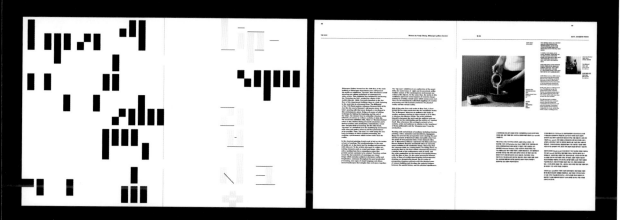

Heritage Tomorrow Project
Book design
2010

Blue Mountains, Flowing Stream
Invitation
2010

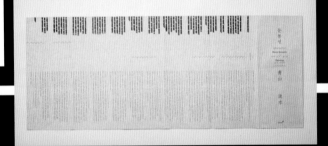

Kumho Museum of Art 20th anniversary exhibition
Exhibition
2009

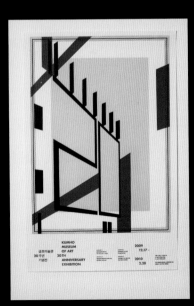

naff 2008 / naff 2009
Event
2008/2009

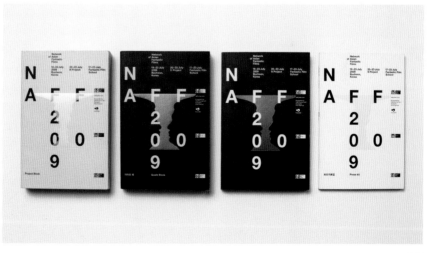

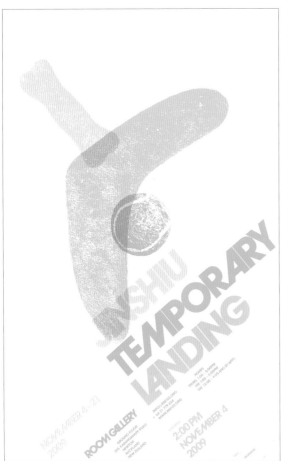

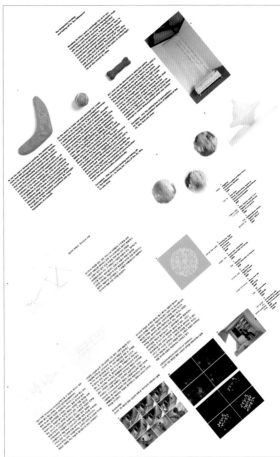

Temporary Landing
Exhibition
2009

Warming Spring and Freezing Fall
Art direction
2008

Xibin Lee
&
Ye Yao

"Many designers try to avoid using Chinese characters because they think it does not look good in typography. But we hope to work out something truly Chinese that we are still doing more study and attempt in this field."

Xinbin Lee and Ye Yao were both born in 1984 and graduated from the Central Academy of Fine Arts in China. They established their own studio established their own studio LEE-YAO STUDIO in 2006. Experimenting with all kinds of Chinese cultural elements in product design and visual communication, they try to convey a truly Chinese mood with their specific design language.

How did you know each other and set up LEE-YAO STUDIO?

In 2007, we collaborated on a project for a competition, by which we won a prize. We felt confident after that so we decided to work on our own and established a self brand.

What is the biggest reward you gain from the brand "Shan-Lin"?

The biggest reward or challenge should be: once you make up your mind to do commercial design, you need to consider everything from design, marketing and sales to finding appropriate clients. We learn to hold a long vision.

Xibin, if Ye Yao were a sound, what would it be?

Pang (the sound of glass breaking), because she is always denying my proposal.

Ye Yao, if Xibin were a shape, what would it be?

A square with a triangle in the bottom, because he is upright yet sophisticated, haha.

Please describe a moment/thing/person that has a strong influence on your work.

Ye Yao: My tutor in the college, Mr. Wang Qipeng, says design is like taking an airplane, you can see the faces of airport staff when you are waiting, but when you

are departed, you can only find large blocks of color of green or blue. Therefore, you need to consider all the matters as a whole, to look in a bird's eye view. And this has become my motto.

Xibin Lee: I attended a torch design team for the 2008 Beijing Olympic Games in 2005, and this project had a great impact on me. I started to understand our traditional culture

and try to remind myself to stay pious when doing design.

What is the wildest/craziest design practice you have done over the years?

In order to persuade a client to accept one of our crazy ideas, we charged nothing in return. There is a lake in a villa in the Beijing suburbia. We wanted to put a chair in the

lake where the water stops people from getting close and sit on it. However, when it comes to winter, the water will freeze and people can get there by walking on the ice. We tried to do a project in combination of nature and time, which makes a design of coming full circle. And that place is so perfect that we just do it without a second hesitation.

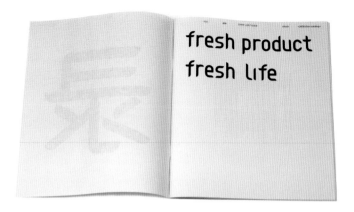

fresh product
fresh life

山林概念
生活品牌
rehpro concept design

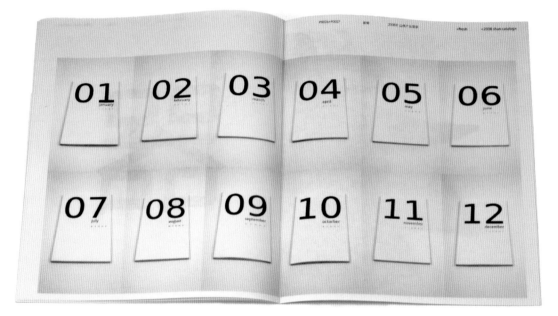

What has been repeatedly used in your artwork?

There are not any particular elements that we keep using in our design I guess, though we are very into Chinese culture and tradition, such as Chinese characters. We applied it on a cushion design and later the monthly bags. Many designers try to avoid using Chinese character because they think it does not look good in typography. But we hope to work out something truly Chinese that we are still doing more study and attempt in this field.

What's the most important to you now?

Health.

Brand Shan
VI
2008

山林概念
生活品牌

(shan) concept design

朴素，单纯，充满生气。

安静的山林中，叶子间意惹的机理的鸣声；泥土中忙碌的脚印气息。山林安静地包容著一切。就像看似安静的山林品牌，朴素地为每个人构建你的生活。

从外表的装扮到内心的延展，每一层的包裹都是内在的一次绽放。这就是服装的美妙之处。

clothes

Simplicity, but full of life.

Quiet in the mountain forest.The sound of leaves; busy footprints in the soil . The mountains quietly contain everything. This is a silent presentation of "shan" brand. "shan"

Dressing people from the outside to the inside. Each layer of dress is a delivery of living attitude. That is the beauty of

Design by LEE-YAO DESIGN STUDIO
Designer LEE CIBIN/YAOYE

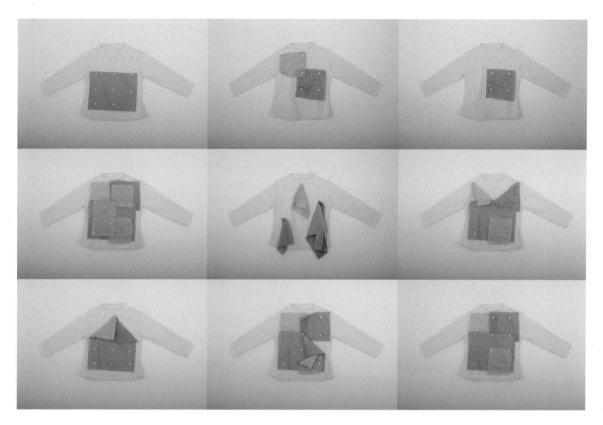

Natural designer
Art direction
2009

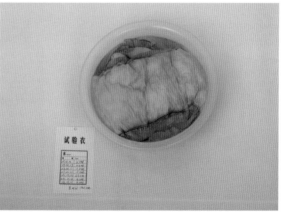

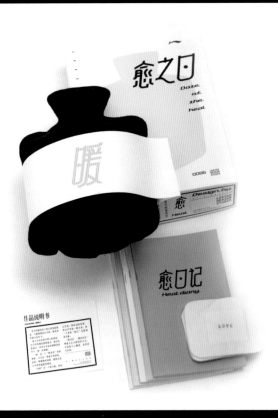

Sole's Story
Product
2007

DUN GALLERY 顿

消防栓
FIRE HYDRANT

DUN Gallery
VI
2009

活动间
ACTIVITY ROOM

男
Gentleman

← 展厅
EXHIBITION HALL

→ 安全出口
EXIT

→ 问询处
INFORMATION

Zaijia Design

After graduating from the Sichuan Fine Arts Institute in June, 1998, Zaijia Huang began a new journey to study and work in France for twelve years. She got her Post diploma (the highest certificate in design) at École nationale supérieure de Arts Décoratifs. Then she began to work for some museums in China, and with the French perfume Kenzo, where a Japanese aesthetic appears in her work. She is currently collaborating with different artists and successfully won projects from Paris Museum of Modern Art, Val De Marne Museum of Contemporary Art and Quai Branly Museum.

Espace Albert Camus
Poster/Editorial
2009

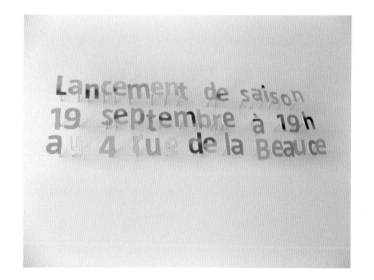

What does a leading-edge designer look like?

A greedy animal playing and jumping among designs to find the extraordinary one. A panda trying to escape from the standard design world.

Jiajia, what does your typical day look like?

Listening, thinking, checking, searching, answering to phone calls, e-mails, ideas, thoughts and whatever.

What is the wildest/craziest design practice you have done over the years?

It was working on the smallest design, not bigger than a rice grain but with many details, and then re-using it in another project to turn into a 25 meters design.

What has been repeatedly used in your artwork?

Designs from the nature, forms and shapes of leafs, flowers, rocks... and cut paper shapes.

What is the best part of being a designer?

While looking for an idea, when I feel that I found something and then close the compute r and start to draw, cut, paste...

A leading-edge designer in your mind? Ask him/her a question.

William Hessel.

-If you could do anything you want, decide everything from the content to the printing, what kind of book would you do?

What distinguishes your work from that of your contemporaries?

My work is very much inspired by ancient objects, stories and art that I translate and use in a contemporary way.

What would you like to be if you were not a designer?

Treasure seeker or archaeologist.

What are you interested in recently?

To develop my design in space (working on exhibition signals).

To develop ideas by turning them into systems that may produce new ideas and designs.

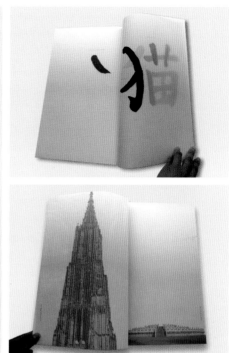

If it was a writing?
Book
2007

*"The best part of being a designer is,
while looking for an idea, when I feel
that I found something and then close the
computer and start to draw, cut, paste..."*

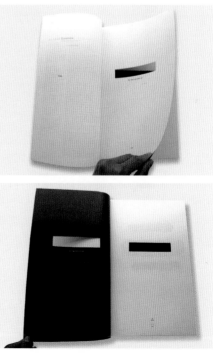

Index

Amsterdam, the Netherlands
Justin Blyth
jblyth.com

Minneapolis, USA
Pure Magenta
www.puremagenta.com

Seoul, Korea
Workroom
workroom.kr

Stockholm, Sweden
Kalle Hagman
www.kallehagman.com

Barcelona, Spain
Raquel Quevedo
www.raquelquevedo.com

Beijing, China
Xibin Lee & Ye Yao
www.s-h-a-n.com

Frankfurt, Germany
Katrin Schacke
www.katrinschacke.de

London, UK
Sawdust
www.madebysawdust.co.uk

Paris, France
Zaijia Design
www.zaijiadesign.com

Paris, France
Les Graphiquants
www.les-graphiquants.fr

Porto, Portugal
Sérgio Alves
www.sergio-alves.com

New York, USA
Mads Jakob Poulsen
www.madsjakobpoulsen.dk

Tokyo, Japan
Shogo Kishino
rokud.com

New York, USA
Mark Pernice
www.maticart.com

Tokyo, Japan
So Hashizume
www.sosososo.com

London, UK
Melvin Galapon
www.mynameismelvin.co.uk

Murcia, Spain
Sublima Comunicación
www.sublimacomunica.com

Beijing/Wuxi, China
more+ studio
erxu.jimdo.com

Melbourne, Australia
Surya Prasetya
www.suryaprasetya.com.au

New York, USA
MyORB
www.myorangebox.com

Dublin, Ireland
Swollen
www.swollen.ie

Tokyo, Japan
Nam
n-a-m.org

Stuttgart, Germany
Tilman Schlevogt
www.tilmanschlevogt.com

Oslo, Norway
Oh Yeah Studio
www.ohyeahstudio.no

Hong Kong, China
Tore Cheung
tearmeboreyou.temptemps.com

Buenos Aires, Argentina
Pablo Alfieri
www.pabloalfieri.com

The Hague, the Netherlands
Trapped in Suburbia
www.trappedinsuburbia.nl

Brussels, Belgium
Pam & Jenny
www.pametjenny.be

Porto, Portugal
Two Dot Two
www.twodotwo.com

Tokyo, Japan
PMKFA
www.pmkfa.com

Emmenbrücke, Switzerland
Typefabric
typefabric.ch

Acknowledgements

We would like to express our gratitude to the artists and designers for their generous contribution of images, ideas and concepts – as well as for sharing their innovation and creativity within these pages. We are very grateful to many other people whose names do not appear in the credits but who provided assistance and support. Without all of you, the creation and ongoing development of this book would not have been possible.